How to Protect Yourself & Survive

From One Woman to Another

HOW TO PROTECT YOURSELF & SURVIVE

From One Woman to Another

Sidney Filson

Photographs by Bert Torchia
Key chain sketches by Jonathan Richards
Striking charts by Jeff Ward

Franklin Watts • New York/London/1979

This book is dedicated to:

YUDA GALAZAN
for returning me to martial art practice
with two working legs;
and to the one master we commonly serve.

The author wishes to thank Simon & Schuster,
Inc. for permission to use an extract from *Against Our Will*
by Susan Brownmiller, published in 1975;
and Linda Lee for permission to use material from *Tao of Jeet Kune Do*
by Bruce Lee, published by Ohara Publications in 1975.

Library of Congress Cataloging in Publication Data

Filson, Sidney.
    How to protect yourself and survive.

    Bibliography: p.
    Includes index.
    1. Self-defense for women. I. Title.
GV1111.5.F54   796.8'1   79-4312
ISBN 0-531-09905-9

Contents

PREFACE
vii

One
I KNOW YOU'RE AFRAID TO PROTECT YOURSELF
3

Two
PREPARING FOR TRAINING
15

Three
WONDER WOMAN SCHOOL, PART I:
BASIC TECHNIQUES
22

Four
WONDER WOMAN SCHOOL, PART II:
BASIC TECHNIQUES
43

Five
WONDER WOMAN SCHOOL, PART III:
EMPTY-HAND COMBINATIONS
65

Six
WEAPONS
79

Seven
HOW TO ACT IN SPECIFIC SITUATIONS
88

Eight
THE ALL-AMERICAN CRIME: RAPE
114

Nine
LIVING ALONE AND LOVING IT
125

Ten
GIVE ME YOUR DAUGHTER AND YOUR MOTHER
130

MY MASTERS, MY MENTORS
142

SUGGESTED READING LIST
145

INDEX
147

Preface

Dear Female Human Being:

I am concerned about your personal safety.

Crime statistics continue to skyrocket, and rape is at an all-time high in rural areas as well as big cities. Regretfully, these days neither Sir Walter Raleigh nor a knight in shining armor are on patrol, ready to aid a damsel in distress.

I understand your fears and confusions about protecting yourself. I'm a woman, and I was bewildered by them too—until I learned *how* to defend myself.

Now, nine years after my introduction to the martial arts, and after training thousands of women to protect themselves, I have written this book to share the benefits of my training and experience with you.

I am going to teach you how to handle yourself successfully in dangerous situations. After you read this book and master its techniques you will have new confidence and need not be afraid to walk alone.

Peace,

Sidney Filson
New York, 1979

How to Protect Yourself & Survive

From One Woman to Another

I Know You're Afraid
to Protect Yourself

It is a sin to let anyone harm the vessel which houses your soul.—Buddha

Your body is a sacred vessel. You have a duty and an obligation to take care of yourself as well as a legal right: self-defense is on the books. So why are women afraid to protect themselves?

Many women think defending themselves means standing toe to toe with an attacker and slugging it out. That's not true. Self-defense is knowing how to protect yourself from harm when you are confronted by danger. The aim of this book is to teach women how to immobilize an attacker with easy, well-placed techniques in order to get out of the danger zone. *Getting away to safety is always the primary objective.*

The reason you are afraid to protect yourself is simply because you don't know how to do it. Think back. I'm sure there was something else in your life that you were afraid of until you learned how to do it. Many people are terrified of diving into the water until they have lessons with a skilled instructor. Driving a car in heavy traffic is scary until you get some on-the-road experience under your belt.

Fear of fighting with an attacker is realistic if you are not trained to do so. Women are afraid to fight men because men fight better. Well, I've got news for you: men are afraid of *women* who know how to fight really well.

I think what might happen to you if you don't defend yourself is what you should be afraid of. The damage done could last for the rest of your life—if there is a rest of your life.

It's up to each woman to learn how to take care of herself in dangerous situations. The streets out there are mean—not just in big cities but all over the country. There are people who would just as soon harm you as not—mug, rape, incapacitate, or murder you. I've had many students who have been attacked in broad daylight on crowded streets and no one has come to their aid. No one.

You don't have to be helpless in the face of attack. You needn't be afraid. You can learn to protect yourself and live the rest of your life without fear.

It makes me angry when I address senior citizen's groups and hear, again and again, "I'm afraid to go to the supermarket for food." And I am thrilled **3** after a good session with women of the same age group who have given me the privilege of training them. Their newly found self-confidence is wonderful to behold. I pity the attacker who faces one of them armed with my key chain weapon. (See chapter six.)

My teaching techniques have been developed especially for women, because I'm a woman. I understand. I went through it all myself. The physical tactics I teach will work for all women—regardless of size, age, and strength—because they require no power. The training patterns are uncomplicated and are easily perfected at home—*as long as* they are practiced conscientiously.

In my eight years of teaching self-defense to women, I've been asked many questions. Before we start training you in self-defense, we should try to answer some of the questions you might ask in a class.

WHY ARE YOU SCARING ME? I DON'T WANT TO THINK ABOUT THINGS LIKE RAPE AND ROBBERY!

Some women become really angry when I give lectures on women's self-defense. They stand up and accuse me of blowing things out of proportion. In such cases, I merely recite the local police statistics—they usually speak for me.

Women who get huffy over the thought of self-defense are the first ones to sign up for a good self-defense class *after* they've had a bad experience.

I'M NOT STRONG. I'VE NEVER BEEN ESPECIALLY ATHLETIC. WILL I BE ABLE TO MASTER YOUR TRAINING TECHNIQUES?

Yes. *None* of my techniques require special strength. All of the techniques in this book have been successfully used by women in their seventies. That's because the only parts of your body that you are going to use are your elbows, knees, heels, the heels of your hands, and your jabbing fingers. These parts of your body are natural weapons. They require no strength to use, only speed and timing, and I will teach you to develop those valuable talents.

WON'T I HURT MY OWN BODY WHEN I DEFEND MYSELF? I'M NOT USED TO CONTACT.

No. The areas of the body I am teaching you to use are not easily hurt. You can go through bricks easily with your elbows and feel nothing! There is a lot of padding on your heels and on the heels of your palms. Hitting a target correctly will bring you no pain. Mother Nature has armed you with natural weapons just like any other animal on this planet. I'm just teaching you to use them.

AM I TOO OLD TO LEARN SELF-DEFENSE?

You are never too old. Even if you are feeble or handicapped you can learn to defend yourself. For example, I will teach you to work with aids—things you already have or which are easily accessible—so you don't have to use your own body. One of the best aids is a key chain as a weapon. It is a tremendous deterrent. It is more effective than an empty hand. A crutch or cane also makes

a marvelous self-defense weapon.

The older you are, the more you need training. The older you are, the more likely you are to be attacked. That's what the statistics show. Face it. Learn how to stop an attack instantly.

IS IT ALWAYS NECESSARY TO FIGHT WHEN THREATENED WITH PHYSICAL VIOLENCE?

No. It is better simply to run away, if possible. Fighting is the last resort.

WON'T GOOD VIBRATIONS AND LOVE STOP ANY VIOLENCE FROM HAPPENING TO ME?

Many women think a soft, reasonable manner can dissuade an attacker from violence. Not true, I'm sorry to say. You can smile and flash peace signs all you want. If someone is going to hurt you, you have a problem.

WON'T AN ATTACKER LEAVE ME ALONE IF I GIVE IN AND DO WHATEVER HE WANTS? ISN'T IT BETTER TO GIVE UP MY MONEY AND JEWELS, OR EVEN BE RAPED, THAN TO FIGHT?

There is no ethical code that says an attacker will *just* rob or rape you. I have seen women horribly mutilated by some nut who thought it would be fun to cut them up *after* robbing and raping them.

If you are armed with self-defense knowledge, at least you have a choice. What you do at your own particular moment of truth is up to you, but I would like to know that you can defend yourself if you want to.

I AM AN INTELLECTUAL PERSON. CAN'T I DEAL ON A DIFFERENT LEVEL AND APPEAL TO THE INTELLECT OF AN ATTACKER?

You could be a mental giant and some intellectual pygmy could rob, kill, or destroy you *physically* because of your lack of knowledge in an area called martial arts. You cannot be truly knowledgeable and omit self-defense training.

WILL SCREAMING GET RID OF AN ATTACKER?

Sometimes, but I would not count on a scream alone to get rid of an attacker. In self-defense, screaming must be accompanied by a good fighting combination. If aid comes as the result of your scream, that's good too. Just don't expect it and you will be pleasantly surprised if it happens.

Screaming is itself a martial-art technique, meant to inflict fear in the heart of your attacker. Soldiers are taught to scream when attacking. Screaming causes confusion; it will give you a moment's advantage—it allows you to strike! The scream you will learn is a full blast from low in the stomach. An advancing woman, screaming and shooting well-placed techniques will terrify a mugger or rapist. It might even discourage him from attacking another woman.

HOW LONG WILL IT TAKE ME TO BE ABLE TO DEFEND MYSELF?

It depends entirely on the amount of time you can put into your training. If you 5 spend twenty-four solid hours on the techniques in this book, practicing faithfully, you will then be capable of using them with good results.

Continuous repetition enables the techniques to become reflexive actions. It also helps you develop a proper power flow. This understanding comes only from repeating the steps many times.

HOW DO I KNOW THAT SELF-DEFENSE TRAINING WILL ENABLE ME TO REACT PROPERLY IN AN EMERGENCY SITUATION?

You will react properly if you train properly. This is why I require you to repeat each training tactic thousands of times. You are being programmed to react in a certain way under attack. You will be working for a purely reflexive response. In an attack situation, there is no time to think—only to react.

You will have to place some trust in the martial art principles that I am teaching. Not reacting properly to danger used to be one of my fears. Then I had the first occasion to defend myself from harmful attack. I don't remember everything I did, but I functioned. I hurt my attacker, and I got away to safety. After it was over I had the shakes. But during the confrontation my martial art training had taken over when needed. So will yours.

WHAT IF I'M ATTACKED AND FEAR PARALYZES ME?

This won't happen if you're prepared. I'm going to teach you how to work *with* your fear, to understand what fear is. Why do you feel immobilized when confronted? There is a simple chemical answer. Fear is nothing more than adrenaline running through your body. This same adrenaline courses through your body when you become angry. For example, you see a growling dog— you become frightened, your adrenaline rises, and the dog smells it. The only way the dog decides whether you are afraid or angry is by your actions. If you retreat, the dog assumes fear and attacks. If you walk forward—an aggressive move—the dog assumes anger and backs off. All adrenaline smells the same because it is the same.

I am going to teach you to work with your adrenaline, making it rise during your training periods so that you will recognize the feeling and be familiar with it. I am going to teach you how to scream. *Screaming enables you to use your adrenaline in a forceful way and rid yourself of fear.*

When you're attacked, you will scream and strike, just like a panther. Your scream will cause paralyzing fear in your attacker. That's another object of screaming. Let the attacker deal with *his* adrenaline while you function as you have been taught.

The breaking down of fear has always been understood by martial artists. We start to deal with fear right at the beginning. You will learn about fear and how to handle it in this book, both physically and psychologically. You'll learn how to direct those fearful feelings out of you and at your attacker, in the form of good strikes accompanied by screams.

6

MOST MEN ARE BIGGER THAN I AM. HOW CAN I POSSIBLY DEFEND MYSELF AGAINST SOMEONE WHO OUTWEIGHS ME BY 100 POUNDS?

Very easily. Remember, you're learning to stop an attack and *get away*. You're not training to stand toe to toe and slug it out with someone twice your size. Also, you must realize that no matter what he weighs, your attacker has vulnerable areas: his knees are still highly kickable and break easily, his eyes and his groin are not protected by his size, and his breathing system is weak— the same as everyone else's. Sometimes being smaller can have its advantages: it's simply a matter of training. Ask any American serviceman who faced a "small" Japanese soldier in hand-to-hand combat during World War II.

ISN'T A LITTLE KNOWLEDGE DANGEROUS—ESPECIALLY WHEN YOU'RE TALKING ABOUT SOMETHING AS SERIOUS AS SELF-DEFENSE?

No. Not if that "little knowledge" is practical, tactical, and deadly! There are many classical tales of martial artists who perfected *one* technique only and were devastating opponents. Don't worry about quantity; go for quality.

It takes years to absorb a lot of knowledge. The martial arts are a lifetime study. You are working with self-defense—immediate protection. You are entirely capable of learning and putting to practical use the techniques in this book. They will work for you. For more extensive study, you must work under an instructor.

IF I BEGIN DEFENDING MYSELF, WON'T IT MAKE MY ATTACKER ANGRY—AND MAKE HIM WANT TO HURT ME MORE?

The attacker can get angry and envision tearing you to pieces. But first he has to deal with the pain you have inflicted on him. That takes time. He may not be able to deal with it at all. He may pass out.

I am going to train you so that you *know* what you are doing. It won't be hit or miss. You aren't going to be delivering halfhearted slaps at his face in the hope that he will go away.

If you fire off a finger jab at an attacker's eyes (see chapter four), there is nothing he can do but grab his eyes and pray for the pain to cease. You are going to learn some devastating defense combinations. After proper execution of them, your assailant is not going to hurt *anyone* for a while.

WON'T AN ATTACKER SEE THAT I AM GOING TO DEFEND MYSELF AND BE ON GUARD?

No. You are going to use the element of surprise. That's your ace in the hole, and you will not let on that you know how to defend yourself. Instead, you will act scared, cry, and plead, "Oh, please don't hurt me...." Then you will seize the opportunity when it arises and strike. His guard will be down. You will see to that.

WHAT IF I CAN'T RUN AWAY FAST ENOUGH?

Don't worry; if you have hit someone where it counts, you will have time. If 7 you have jabbed your finger in somebody's eye, there is nothing he can do except hold his eye and scream. He must deal with both the pain and impaired vision.

Anywhere I teach you to strike is going to immobilize your attacker. And you will be using *combinations* of devastating strikes. We are going to work only on weak areas of the human body: head (computer); breathing system (compressor); legs (suspension system). Perhaps if you think about it this way you will see how little you have to worry about once you have committed yourself to defense.

WHAT IF SOMEONE ATTACKS ME FROM BEHIND?

You will learn how to defend yourself from the rear, either with your empty hand or with a weapon (the key chain). We're going to cover every possible situation in which you can be accosted. I am going to teach you, step by step, how to handle an assailant who comes at you from behind, from the side, and from head on. We will also deal with specific locations—the street, a car, an elevator, your home—wherever you may be in danger.

WHAT IF I GET KNOCKED DOWN BY A SURPRISE ATTACK?

This is a possibility. No matter how much training a person has, it is possible to be caught unaware. I'll teach you exactly how to fall so you won't get hurt yet will be prepared to defend yourself the minute you hit the ground.

Ground fighting is deadly and easy, even if you're dizzy from a blow. Remember, if someone knocks you down, he still has to approach your person to harm you. This is what you wait for. You will learn to be prepared.

I'M FRIGHTENED OF THE LOUD CURSING AND FOUL LANGUAGE THAT AN ATTACKER COULD SHOUT AT ME. HOW COULD I HANDLE THAT?

Many women are scared to death of full-volume foul expletives, but you must realize that, as offensive as the words may be, they are only *words* and cannot harm you. The attacker is using his own kind of "yell of spirit" by shouting at you. It is both a way to frighten you and a means of bolstering his own courage.

I will teach you a specific kind of breathing to use in this situation. This breathing will calm you so that you can think clearly and prepare to deal with the physical attack. That's what you have to worry about!

AT WHAT EXACT MOMENT SHOULD I STRIKE TO DEFEND MYSELF? DO I WAIT TO GET HIT? SHOULD I STRIKE AFTER A THREAT?

There are several different answers, depending upon the circumstances. If you knew for sure that a person were going to harm you (i.e., if you had just seen him kill someone), you should strike at the first opportunity.

If someone were screaming curses at you, he might be making empty threats, and you should be alert, but wait to see what his next move would be.

If you sensed that someone was following you down a dark street (or any street) it would be a good bet that he intended to accost you. Therefore you should formulate your strategy for handling him, and even lure him into a position of advantage to you.

We will cover all the possibilities specifically. Don't worry. You will learn the exact moment to strike.

BUT COULDN'T AN ATTACKER SEEK REVENGE ON A WOMAN WHO HAS SUCCESSFULLY DEFENDED HERSELF IN THE INITIAL CONFRONTATION?

Deal with each threat as it arises. Otherwise you will live your life in fear. Don't worry about the future. What could a returning attacker do to you that would be worse than what he had done the first time?

Dealing with the initial attack will get you instant respect. He knows you can defend yourself, and there are many easier marks out there for him to pick on. The attacker who gets away with the initial rape or robbery or beating is the one who's likely to come back for more.

For example, here's a story from my collection of actual encounters:

Big City, U.S.A., 8:30 P.M. Jean was sitting on her bed, hairdryer humming away on her head as she concentrated on applying nail polish. Suddenly, there was a man standing over her. The intruder threw her back on the bed, and with the hairdryer still blasting away he raped her.

It was over as suddenly as it started, and Jean was left alone, in a state of shock and horror: "The only thing I could think of was to get clean. I remember glancing at the bedroom window, seeing it open, and noting that he must have come up the fire escape. Calling the police didn't even enter my mind. I'd heard so many bad reports of women who had reported rape. I ran a bath and was sitting in the tub when he returned. He pulled me out of the tub, threw me down on the bathroom floor, and raped me again! I was hysterical when I called the police. They did not believe my story and asked if I had been parading around naked in front of open windows."

Jean went to a hotel that night. Friends packed up her belongings. She never returned to that apartment and moved to a new neighborhood. She also became one of my students.

If Jean had defended herself in the first place, the rapist would never have come back.

WHAT SHOULD I DO IF I'M CONFRONTED BY MORE THAN ONE PERSON?

Decide immediately who is the leader, the strongest. He is the one you must confront. If a group is coming at you, I hope you have your key chain with you. The circles you can make will form a moving umbrella of protection for you.

I once had a hair-raising encounter with a group. I was teaching martial arts in a run-down neighborhood. My car was parked in a lot. It was dark. I passed a group of boys, aged twelve to about sixteen, sitting on some steps. They whistled, made catcalls and goading comments as I went by. I ignored them and continued to my car. When I reached it, I leaned toward the door to open

9

Watch out for groups.

Deal with the leader only.

it with the key and saw the reflection of those boys fanning out and forming a circle behind me.

At that time *nunchakas*[1] were legal in New York State. I had a beautiful pair in my backpack, the ends sticking out and available, right where they belonged. I had been practicing with them that day.

Whenever I see big trouble coming I talk silently to myself; it seems to help. I called for God's help in my martial art manner and reached for my *nunchakas*. They made a lot of noise (they were made of plexiglass and chain) as I whirled to face my opponents. My weapon was in ready position, my breathing under control; adrenaline was racing through my system.

The gang faded sheepishly away. Whether it was the noise of my weapon, my crazy-eyed, weird, smiling face, or the fact that the gang recognized my weapon from the popular Bruce Lee films—or a combination of the three—I have no idea. The anticlimactic effect was so strong that I stood there for quite a while, getting myself together in order to drive my car.

If I had shown fear of any sort I am sure they would have attempted rape. Young teenage gangs are totally unreasonable and mainly concerned with impressing each other. There were quite a few of them, and the situation could have been horrible.

The key chain weapon I will teach you to use is capable of circular movements exactly like *nunchakas*. It is also constructed to make noise, always a good psychological ploy for you. A police whistle dangling at the end of the key chain is also good to use under group attack.

Here is another technique which will stop whole crowds: *go insane.* Dribble from the mouth; do a Quasimodo. Forget how you look; you must pretend to go berserk or to have a fit. (*Don't* throw yourself onto the ground though—never do that!) History books describe how village idiots survived after everyone else went to meet their maker. Everyone is afraid of insanity. Pretending to go insane is a technique which you can use to your advantage.

WHAT ABOUT DEALING WITH SOMEONE WHO IS UNDER THE EFFECTS OF ALCOHOL OR NARCOTICS? IS THERE A SPECIFIC WAY TO COPE WITH THEM?

Yes, definitely. Someone who is drunk or stoned presents a special problem psychologically. Physically, he may be easier to deal with because his balance is precarious, and he's easy to knock off his feet. I will deal very specifically with this area of self-defense, so you will know *exactly* how to handle it.

BUT WHAT IF I HURT SOMEBODY?

It may be necessary to inflict pain on an attacker. Go ahead and hurt him. He's probably going to hurt you if you don't.

---

[1]*Nunchakas*, two sticks joined together with a rope or chain, are capable of enormous devastation and are illegal in most states—falling into the same classification as guns. Made popular by Bruce Lee movies, *nunchakas* are actually an Okinawan rice-chaffing tool converted into a weapon by oppressed peasant farmers.

Make your choice: who's worth more to you? You—or someone you don't know who is trying to rob you, use you, and possibly cut you up or kill you?

Your main objective is to defend yourself and get away. There is no time to pause even for a second to see how badly you have hurt your assailant.

IT IS AGAINST MY RELIGION TO FIGHT. WHAT SHOULD I DO?

Accept your fate. You are in God's hands.

SHOULD I PROTECT OTHERS?

I say, yes! If you are trained in self-defense and see an opportunity to help another human out of a pickle, go ahead. When women come to me to train in a group, I tell them they are now *dojo* sisters. They have become responsible for each other's safety. (A dojo is the temple-gym where martial arts are practiced.)

An hysterical mother once came to me. While riding a crowded subway car in mid-afternoon, her thirteen-year-old daughter had been accosted. She was sitting, minding her own business, when an adult male stood directly in front of her and, in full view of everyone on the crowded subway car, exposed himself and forced the young girl to commit an act of oral sex. No one helped that child!

The girl was so traumatized by the experience that she refused to go to school and would not communicate with anyone. Her desperate mother had tried church and psychiatric counseling, to no avail.

We were lucky. She responded to me and to self-defense training. I know

You can
*come to
someone's aid.*

12

that now my student can take care of herself. That horrible incident will not be repeated because she can personally stop it, without outside help.

I know something else. There is no way I could have been on that subway car without helping that child. I would expect any student of mine to do the same. It's time for a change in attitude. The horror story of the woman in New York City who was murdered while thirty passive people watched must never be repeated.

If you study martial arts in any form—and self-defense is definitely a part of the martial arts—you are bound to use your art to stand up for what is right.

SHOULD I BUY A GUN?

You certainly should learn how to use one. Most men know how to operate firearms; most women do not. Most criminals have guns; most women do not.

If there is a gun in your home you should know how to operate it. This includes knowing how to maintain the weapon and keep it in operable condition.

Most states allow registered hunting guns in the home. Some states allow handguns. Check your local laws. Find out what's legal for you.

If you live in an area where you feel threatened by firearms, it is my opinion that you should have the same weapons available for your own defense. This is certainly your own choice, but don't be an ostrich about it. Don't bury your head to avoid the issue.

HOW YOUNG CAN MY DAUGHTER START SELF-DEFENSE TRAINING?

Six years old. Before then, most children lack the concentration needed for serious classes. This training involves a great deal of discipline; it's not just learning the motions.

WON'T SELF-DEFENSE CLASSES FOR CHILDREN MAKE THEM AFRAID? AREN'T THEY TOO YOUNG TO DEAL WITH SUCH HARSH REALITIES?

No. Your children will be aware, not afraid. I hope your child hasn't had a problem and never will. But you would worry a lot less if you knew your children could defend themselves against attack.

WHAT IF MY MAN OBJECTS TO HAVING ME LEARN SELF-DEFENSE?

This is common. A lot of men object to having females learn to protect themselves. Perhaps they feel it is threatening to their masculinity. If a woman can protect herself, then the man is not needed. Here are some valid arguments to throw his way:

Cite the aristocratic Samurai culture. The women were genteel and feminine yet could fight side by side with their men.

Even if your man is a wonderful fighter and could defend you against all attackers, ask him what you are supposed to do when he's not around? Is he aware of the statistics? Does he know that if you live in a highly populated area you are more likely than not to have some sort of confrontation? (Use these

13

same arguments if he objects to having his daughter learn to defend herself.)

You can also choose not to tell anyone that you are learning self-defense. Just gather knowledge and store it away for emergency use. This is something personal you're doing for yourself, by yourself. Ideally, you should not tell *anyone* that you know how to defend yourself. (Many rapes are classified as "friendly rapes:" someone you know just walks all over you.) This is your secret. Keep it to yourself. Your advantage always lies in the element of surprise.

WON'T I APPEAR MASCULINE IF I LEARN SELF-DEFENSE?

No—to the contrary, this training builds grace and agility. The body movements you are learning are similar to dance. The only difference is that you are combining movement with focused power.

I don't feel robbed of my feminity. Instead, my training has contributed to my life as a woman. Take a look at the women pictured in this book. They are all my students, either in self-defense or karate. Do they appear masculine?

BUT WON'T I DEVELOP A MASCULINE ATTITUDE?

My answer would have to be yes: if defending your human rights and your person is considered exclusively masculine; if saying "no" firmly and meaning it is masculine; if being totally independent and capable of handling yourself in any situation is masculine.

IS IT REALLY NECESSARY FOR ME TO LEARN ALL OF THIS?

Civilization has encouraged the male to learn how to use physical violence—and the female to accept it. You, as a female, have choices. Stand up and fight, or accept being prey. What else is there? Laws cannot prevent damage; they can only punish a perpetrator *after* you have been harmed. Does that satisfy you?

If you want to know how to protect yourself, you cannot make a light pass at self-defense. You must be prepared to deal with sudden changes, anything unexpected, at a moment's notice. For this you must be prepared mentally and physically. This book includes what I feel in good conscience is necessary for proper self-defense; remember, you are not training to win at hand-to-hand combat; you are learning to stop an attack and get away.

14

Preparing for Training TWO

DISCIPLINE AND THE CULTIVATION OF "IRON WILL"

Only through practice and discipline will you succeed in learning from this book. Don't delude yourself into thinking a light pass at these techniques will prepare you for actual confrontations. You must set aside a specific period of time to work on your self-defense techniques and never deviate from that set period. I would suggest no less than one half-hour at least three times per week. If you are seriously interested in learning these self-defense techniques, you will work every day.

It's your choice, but I do hope you will start each workout by chanting a set of virtues and doing a warm-up. (See sections on virtues and warm-ups in this chapter.) That way you will be physically and mentally prepared for your training.

If self-discipline has been a problem in the past, don't worry; you can change. There is no better way to turn over a new leaf than by practicing the martial arts. When you feel about to waver, to give in to less than perfection, remember this slogan:

LET'S GO! KEEP GOING! THERE IS NOTHING ELSE!

Use it. Print it in large letters, and hang it where you work out. Glancing at it will remind you to be disciplined, always to complete your task.

If I were teaching you in person, in my class, instruction would be conducted with military discipline. There would be no talking, no break for any reason: not fatigue, frustration, telephone calls, nor to go to the bathroom. None of these reasons would impress an attacker if you were defending your life: "Oh, I can't fight back now, I have to go to the bathroom" or, "Excuse me, could you attack me later, I'm tired now?"

It will be harder for you, at home, because there is no instructor standing over you. You're going to have to do it yourself. But you *can* do it! This self-imposed discipline will be the best thing you ever did for yourself. I promise. The sense of accomplishment you will feel after working out on a day when you're tired or just feeling lazy will make up for it all. You will be a stronger woman because of it.

So, for your own sake and for the development of your self-defense, set the clock; work out by that clock. Do not deviate. In karate it is called "building the iron will." That is what I want you to do.

Take a Test of Pain

If you would like to see how much iron will you have, what stuff you are really made of, and if you want the slightest hint of what it is like to make contact knuckle to target, take a test of pain. Try knuckle push-ups.

Make a strong fist by rolling up your fingers very tightly and holding the fingers together with your thumb. Now place your fists on the floor, (your palms should face each other) and support your entire body on the first two knuckles only. (You may put a towel down to avoid breaking the skin.) Do not pay attention to the pain and do push-ups!

The reason martial artists do so many knuckle push-ups is to toughen the knuckles for punching. After enough work, no pain is felt when making contact with a target. This book's self-defense training does not require these push-ups. I thought it would be interesting for you to test your pain tolerance.

BODY CONDITIONING

Remember, the first order of self-defense is to run away if possible. Now, if you're jogging as a hobby that's an easy order. If you're badly out of shape, you have no choice: you have to stand and fight.

It is best to have a well-conditioned heart and body. Many women are out of shape only because they have never learned how to eat and exercise properly. *It is never too late to get in tip-top physical condition.* I have shaped up women in their sixties with excellent results. There is no reason for your body to fall apart as you grow older. Learning self-defense does not require a full body-conditioning program. But I would rather see you in peak shape. I hope you feel the same way.

If you were undertaking a full martial arts program, I would have you in high-level physical condition in three months, no matter how out of shape you are. You would be able to run a mile or jump rope for fifteen minutes without being winded, stretch for a half hour, do twenty-five knuckle push-ups, then begin to work on technique and form. You would be very strong. Your diet would be 80 percent raw food.

If you are serious about changing your shape and improving your health, try my jump-rope program and raw food diet in *Jump Into Shape*.[1] You'll feel like a million dollars!

Upper-Body Conditioning

Most women lack upper-body strength. According to Sue Peterson,

[1]Sidney Filson and Claudia Jessup, *Jump Into Shape* (Franklin Watts, Inc., 1978).

*Sue Peterson
watches Filson
demonstrate
at West Point.*

women's self-defense instructor at West Point, when the academy admitted
women to the cadet programs for the first time, the upper-body physical
standards had to be dropped way down. Although all the women cadets were
considered athletic by their high schools, none of them could do push-ups and
chin-ups.

Women are not taught to do strength-building exercises, and the result is an
unbalanced, sick body. The lack of upper-body use in a woman's life
contributes to arthritis, rounding of the shoulders (widow's hump), and
hanging flesh on upper arms. These warning signals start to occur at about
thirty-five, younger in some cases. These painful, ugly distortions do not have
to happen. Your palm heel strikes (chapter three) will help to overcome this
weakness. But I would suggest doing more to insure strong upper-body
muscles. Men don't have these particular problems, because they are used to
lifting heavy objects and using their upper bodies on a regular basis.

Jumping rope helps a lot. Push-ups are the best single exercise for the upper
body that I could possibly give you. Swimming the crawl (freestyle) is excellent.

Here's a great home aid: hang a chinning bar in the doorway to the kitchen.
Make a house rule: every time you go into the kitchen, do a pull-up;
every time you leave the kitchen, do a pull-up. It may take you a while to do
full pull-ups, but time will take care of that, and you'll burn up some extra
calories on the bar. Once you are able to do either push-ups or pull-ups, you
will see a wonderful difference in your upper body: firm arms, rounded chest,
shapely back and neck.

HOW TO USE THE TECHNIQUE CHAPTERS
*Work on the techniques in the order in which they are presented in the
following chapters.* The techniques are arranged in a logical order for the
beginning self-defense student. Trust me and follow that order. If you jump
around and go to advanced techniques first, you will outsmart yourself.

17

Work on a technique until you can do all your variations and requirements without referring to the written instructions. Don't rush it. Once you, or you and your partner, have reached this point, it should not take you long to complete one technique workout. Then it is time to go on to the next technique.

Start each workout with your newest technique. Work out, referring to the written instruction if you have to, then go on to the techniques you know and whiz through them. Keep adding to your repertoire in this way. Don't take on a new technique until you are sure of the ones you're working on.

Reread your general rules for practicing basics often and make sure your technique meets all the requirements listed there.

After working on a new technique for the first time, reread the instructions. Since I'm not with you to catch your mistakes and give you a "well done" when you're on the money, you're going to have to run a constant check on yourself.

If you proceed in this fashion you will build a firm base of self-defense techniques and reach the point where you can do a total workout of all the strikes and kicks taught in this book in one session.

Once you have absorbed all the techniques you can vary your workouts. For instance, one day you could concentrate on becoming very fast and just do full-speed work. Another day, you might work on just one technique, repeating it hundreds and hundreds of times. (I set high numbers of repetitions for myself when I'm not satisfied with my performance.) At another time, you might like to work just on your legs. You could be dissatisfied with your left leg and hand techniques and spend a whole week working on nothing but your left side. (That makes a lot of sense for right-sided people and vice-versa.)

Remember, once you have learned the mechanics of the techniques you cannot stop working on them. In order to have your weapons (techniques) at the ready you must keep them in tip-top shape. That means working out regularly to keep up form and speed levels.

BASIC RULES OF PRACTICE

Work for Perfect Form

Your self-defense will work only if your form is perfect! That means you must pay attention to the tiniest things. If you sense that you are doing something wrong, correct it. (See "Breaking Bad Habits," in chapter four.) Make it perfect. Otherwise all your work is for naught. Precision practice is required. Set high standards and you will succeed.

There is great reward in achieving perfection of form: a feeling of being "poetry in motion." You'll know when it happens, and precision equals accuracy.

Always Work in Slow Motion First

This will allow you to relax and concentrate on your form. Remember, you must have perfect form! That is the only way these techniques will work for you. I want you to be really picky about your form. You must even pay attention to where your pinky finger is during hand work.[2] I want you to be totally aware of every little thing you are doing. *Only slow-motion* work will bring you this awareness. Relax and learn.

Working with Mirrors Is Wonderful for You

Always try to position yourself in front of a mirror while working out; in that way, you can observe and correct yourself.

Body Stillness Is Important

When you are working on a hand technique, move only that part of the body—no other. This will require your strongest concentration—excellent mind training for you. This rule holds true for every move you learn.

Center Your Technique

Everything you learn will require you to work on your own center line. Foot or hand strike, elbow or knee, you are still going to concentrate on the line that extends directly forward from your solar plexus. It is your power line; your energies flow freely on this line. Find it on your own body. The center line runs from your nose to your groin. *All techniques must radiate from this center line.* Even the slightest deviation to the right or left of the power line means loss of effectiveness for your technique.

Do All the Repetitions Required

Always complete your technique count. This will be your discipline: do not deviate.

Working with a Partner

If you can get a buddy to work with you, learning self-defense will be easier. It is always better to have an actual body to grip and work with. The most valuable thing you will learn is how close you need to be to strike a vulnerable area. When partners work together, they can aid each other by being very critical and picking up mistakes.

Be disciplined when working with a partner. Don't let your workout turn into a gab session; work straight through. Start with your basic workout; then go on to your partner work. If you are studying the advanced teaching chapters, you will work on your combinations.

If your partner is female, take into consideration that an attacker would probably be taller and heavier. As long as you train your eyes to see the striking point, you'll hit it whatever the size of the attacker.

If you don't have a partner, imagine one. You can sink knee strikes into pillows and do a lot of other improvising. I have a student who tells me she has beaten up all her furniture practicing at home.

---

[2]If your pinky finger were hanging out instead of being closed, and you had to fight, it might hook on a piece of your attacker's clothing and break. You would still have to defend yourself and with the added burden of a painful, broken finger.

Do not be discouraged if you do not understand a move at first. Just keep practicing. The light of understanding will dawn, I promise you. It may take many repetitions of a technique before real comprehension comes to you.

YOUR "YELL OF SPIRIT"

You will notice that every technique I'm teaching you in this book is accompanied by a "yell of spirit," a martial art scream. Once you begin working and screaming you will be amazed at the energy boost you experience. When you stop working you won't be able to hold your hand steady if you put it out in front of you. These are good healthy shakes, produced by adrenaline. Your whole body comes alive with it.

Do not be reluctant to scream while doing full-speed work. Many of my students find the yell of spirit embarrassing at first. So did I. I got over that feeling and so will you. If you don't scream when you practice, your scream won't come automatically when you are under pressure, and *screaming is of major importance*. A scream is a weapon in itself. A scream causes confusion and panic in an attacker—exactly what you want! A scream *may* bring help (it's a small chance—but why overlook it).

Screaming will help you deal with your natural fear! The tremendous surge of adrenaline that courses through your body in an emergency situation must be directed outward at your opponent. In order to release this chemical fear (adrenaline), scream. The scream will boost your power. Trust me and make sure you scream with every full-speed technique you throw.

This yell of spirit is meant to strike terror into the heart of your opponent.

An old martial art tale tells of a master who developed his *keyiii* (yell of spirit) by holding small animals in his hand and killing them with his scream! This story will help you to understand the intensity required for a good yell of spirit.

Just make sure your scream comes from deep within your gut. If you can make the sound strange and scary, all the better. If you ever have the opportunity to catch a Bruce Lee movie,[3] note the weird, high-pitched, nerve-wracking sound Master Lee makes as he fights.

Remember the blasting of a police siren. Our society has taught people to fear loud piercing sounds and to freeze upon hearing them. Take advantage of that already instilled fear factor; use your yell of spirit.

Screaming during practice will be good for you in other ways. There are psychological therapies (Primal Scream is one) which use screaming to release tension. After a session of practicing your self-defense and using your yell of spirit, you will find that your troubles seem fewer, your problems easier to deal with.

If you live in an apartment, and it is impossible for you to give vent to a full-volume scream, you must use the quiet yell of spirit. Every time you throw a strike, give a "whispered scream" from low in the stomach. You must use the

[3]*Enter the Dragon, Fist of Fury, Return of the Dragon, Green Hornet TV Series.*

yell of spirit no matter what the circumstances, even if you have to muffle it. It is supremely important for your self-defense development.

WARMING UP

I'm not expecting you to go into a full athletic program, but I do want you to warm up for the sake of your muscles (you don't want to pull them) and circulation. If you are an athletic person, just add self-defense training to your existing program. If you have been leading a sedentary life, I will give you a choice of three easy warm-ups to precede your workout. Use one or all to avoid boredom: 100 jumping jacks, 100 jumps with a jump rope, running in place for the count of 200.

Jumping jacks and jumping rope are preferable to running in place because you use your upper body and get optimum warm-up. But each of the above will do the job and get you heated up enough to start training. I like to do all of these warm-ups to disco beat music as it helps liven up the pace.

If you are really out of shape, start out with twenty-five and increase the number until you build to the correct count.

Stretching for a few minutes after the warm-up will guarantee better muscle tone. Just lean over and touch your toes while keeping your legs straight. Stay there and breathe in and out quietly for a full minute. Come up, take a deep breath, and go into the toe-touching stretch for another minute. You should feel refreshed, warm, stretched, and ready to learn how to protect yourself and survive.

YOUR VIRTUES

Stand straight or, better yet, kneel in a position of meditation. Place your hands in your lap, let the ends of your thumbs touch each other, close your eyes, and repeat these virtues out loud. If you are working in a group, one person should say a line, then the group should repeat that line as one voice, then on to the next line, and so forth. Your virtues should be the very beginning of your workout, even before your warm-up:

THE MARTIAL ARTS ARE MY SECRET, I BEAR NO ARMS
MAY GOD HELP ME IF I EVER HAVE TO USE MY ART
I SHALL FIND MY STRENGTH AS A WOMAN
I SHALL ALWAYS BE AWARE
I SHALL BE QUICK TO SEIZE OPPORTUNITY
NOTHING IS IMPOSSIBLE

And, with your virtues in mind, undertake a serious workout. Do not allow any disturbances. Say your virtues again, at the end of your practice, then remain quiet for a few moments of meditation.

LET'S GO!

Say your virtues, do a warm-up, and start your palm heel strikes.

21

THREE Wonder Woman School, Part I: Basic Techniques

YOUR PRACTICE STANCE

Stand with your toes pointed forward your feet your own shoulders' width apart for good balance. Not narrower, not wider. *Always flex your knees.* This will assure a strong, well-balanced stance and will condition your legs. Bending at the knees helps you to feel the earth. As you progress in your training you will realize that much of your power comes from the strength of your stance. *Grip the ground with your toes.* This is possible with or without shoes. One can develop a special feeling for the ground. Keep your toes together and be aware of them; their gripping power is like that of a rubber tire gripping the road. Be relaxed in your shoulder-width stance. It is an easy one.

If your legs feel tired while you are practicing, bend your knees more. Sink even lower into the shoulder-width stance, as if you were sitting. This is good for your legs and your discipline. Don't relieve your legs by straightening up, instead—go *down more.* Finish whatever you are working on; then you may straighten up.

PALM HEEL STRIKE

To be practiced in the shoulder-width stance with hands in the open-chamber position at your rib cage. Make sure your fingers are together. Pull your hands back as far as you can. (This position will feel strange at first.) Make sure your elbows are directly behind your hands, not out to the sides.

22

1. *Move your right hand forward and toward the center of your body.* Keep the edge of your palm *hard against your rib cage.* Then the edge of your wrist *presses against your rib cage.* Then, the forearm presses *hard against the rib cage.* Your hand should now be directly in front of your solar plexus (on the center line of your body), traveling slowly forward on that line. Keep going forward. Now your elbow should be *pressed hard against your rib cage. As the elbow passes the rib cage, your hand must turn.* Your fingers must point upward, and the edge of your palm (the palm heel) is pushed forward. Keep going until the arm is at full extension, leaving a small flex in the elbow. Make sure the strike is centered and no higher than shoulder level. Your shoulders should be kept back and still. Only your palm heel travels forward.

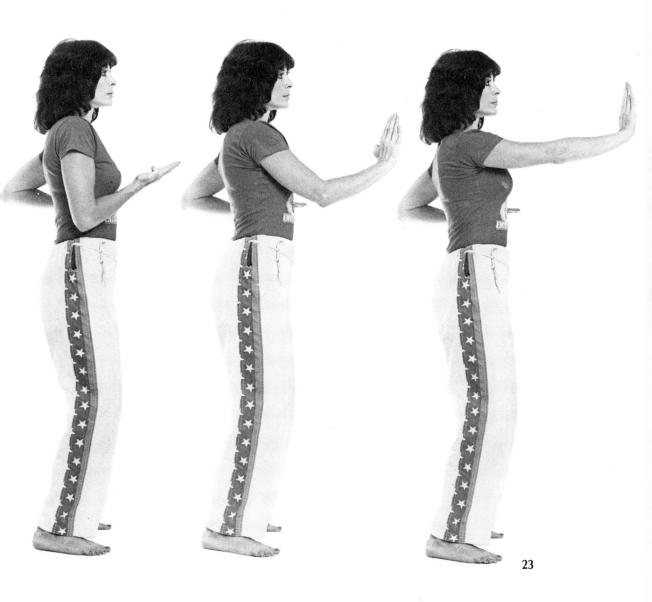

2. *Alternate hands.* As your left hand starts moving slowly forward and seeking the center line of your body, your right hand will move slowly back. Both hands must stick close to the rib cage. Both hands must turn at the same time. Now your left hand will be executing the palm heel strike while your right hand returns to the chamber position, palm upward, fingers closed.

Repeat fifty times in slow motion. Develop a fluid, flowing motion as you alternate your hands. Relax your knees, flexing them a bit. Keep your shoulders back. Concentrate only on the form. Seek the center line of your body; *stick to your rib cage.*

Repeat fifty times at full speed, screaming with each strike. Make sure the yell of spirit comes deep from your lower stomach; *throw a strong sound.* As you throw fast palm heel strikes you will begin to realize that the power is coming from your feet and your hips, not your shoulders. Settle into that flexed-knee stance. Make sure your elbow remains flexed—don't snap it! Most important of all, make sure your strikes are centered on your middle line, no higher than your own shoulder height. Always return to chamber faster than you went out, so you are ready to use your weapon again (like cocking a gun), and no one can grab your hand.

The palm heel strike has many variations, each with its own uses. You can turn it sideways (for rib and kidney strikes) and upside down (for a groin blow). You can use both hands at the same time, for double devastation.

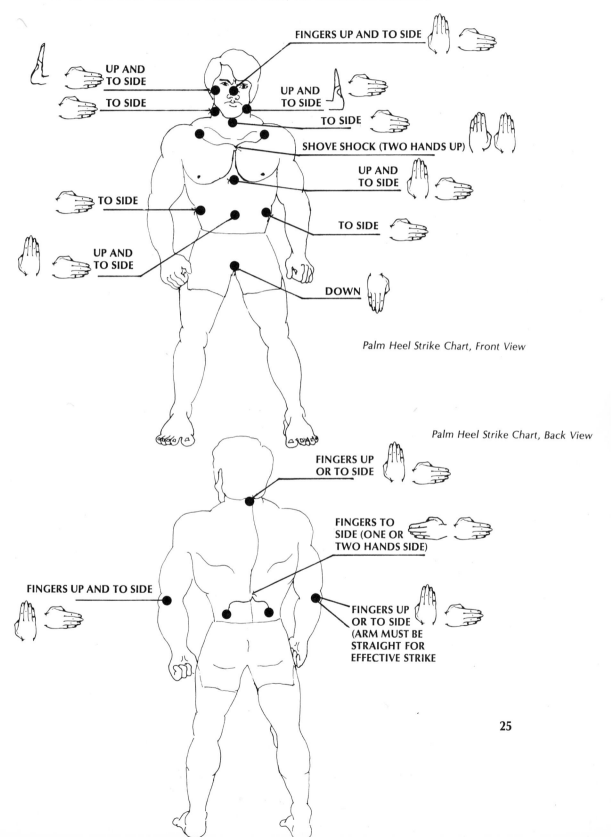

Palm Heel Strike Chart, Front View

Palm Heel Strike Chart, Back View

*Double palm
heel strike
to kidneys.*

Double Palm Heel Strike

A double palm heel strike is executed the same as single palm heel strike. *Both hands move forward at the same time; both hands turn as both elbows pass the rib cage.* You may strike with palms in and fingers to the side, or you may contact your target with hands side by side, fingers up. (Spread your hands apart a bit and you're set for shove shock.)

1. *Strike with fingers to the side* (for kidney, solar plexus, low stomach, and throat).

Repeat twenty-five times in slow motion.

Repeat twenty-five times at full speed with a loud yell of spirit.

2. *Strike with fingers up* (shove shock, striking two attackers in the face at the same time, or striking under both sides of the chin).

Repeat twenty-five times in slow motion.

Repeat twenty-five times at full speed with a loud yell of spirit.

Make sure you come back to chamber swiftly. Don't leave your strikes on target!

If you strike upward and contact your opponent under the chin with one or both palm heels, he will suffer a whiplash injury,[1] temporarily paralyzing his upper body and making it difficult for him to bother you further. If you've ever had your head snapped back suddenly, you know the feeling. It is immobilizing, shocking, and painful, all at once!

---

[1]This injury may be either permanent or temporary—the same as a whiplash injury resulting from a snapped head in a car accident.

Directed straight into and slightly under the solar plexus, the palm heel will play havoc with an attacker's breathing system. It will stop him. A good shot will knock him out. If you've ever fallen off a horse you know what I'm talking about. Getting hit in the breathing system with the palm heel knocks the wind out of you. Collecting oneself after such a blow takes time. (Time when you can get away.)

Delivered to the front-center of the face, this strike will cause terrific pain to the nose, and the eyes will water and blur. A palm heel strike delivered to the side-center of the face is also devastating. Never leave your palm heel on its target—always bring it back to chamber.

A quick palm heel thrust to the front-center of the throat (windpipe) is unbelievably effective. (Just make sure the attacker's chin is up, exposing enough throat striking space to give a clear opening, for your palm heel to fit.) Give a little tap to your own windpipe. See how sensitive it is? Imagine a fully-practiced, well-placed palm heel strike in that vulnerable area.

You can place full confidence in the palm heel strike. It is devastating, and properly executed it won't hurt the bottom of your palm, your hand, or your elbow.

I was a member of a class where the instructor would walk the lines as we sweated and threw our palm heel strikes; "What is your target point for the palm heel strike?" he would yell.

"The back of the skull" we screamed at the top of our lungs in programmed unison.

"How do you get there?" was his next full-volume question.

"Through the front of the face" was the class rejoinder. Not the most pleasant thought, but the concept is valid.

It is very important for you to realize fully how powerful this strike is and how much stopping-power it contains. That's the only way you will have full confidence in it and feel free to use your palm heel for self-defense.

Another terrific advantage is that you're throwing this strike straight out from your center. People don't expect that. Most guys swing a punch around in a hooking manner, and that's what they expect in return. You've got a little surprise for an attacker—a neat straight-lined technique. They'll never be able to figure out where it came from! That's what women need—tricks up their sleeves.

Don't rack your brain over understanding the palm heel strike right now. Just practice it exactly as I've described it. Don't change anything, and do all of your repetitions. You may find yourself testing the strike. I used to try to hit things with my palm heel when I was learning. I was afraid I might hurt myself if I really had to use it. But the first time I had to break a board, I used the palm heel strike and was surprised when the board fell apart like butter!

Work for a solid week on the palm heel strike. If I were training you personally, I would repeat this information many times. Since I can't stand over you, you'll have to read my words over and over again. One day you'll really understand this technique and relate to its use. Don't be impatient. Work hard; it'll pay off!

27

Shove Shock with Palm Heels

Peter Urban, Grand Master of U.S.A. GoJu karate teaches a special technique to his women students. He calls it "shove shock," and says, "I've had women knock men literally on their ass, by emphasizing a sudden shoving and shocking, as opposed to punching, which takes more power development."

Master Urban feels that shove shock is particularly suited to women, much as claw fighting is suited to cats. Punching, for men, he compared to dog biting. "No dog can beat a cat, on a pound-for-pound level." The master feels that this shove shock technique is a great leveler for women.

To execute shove shock, strike with both palm heels at the same time just below the attacker's shoulders. Make sure the placement of your palm heels is just *under* the top of his shoulders. You wouldn't want your palm heels to slip over. It is always important to use this technique suddenly. By hitting the wide upper part of the body, your strikes cause a "bowling over" action.

Warning—As in all techniques, make sure you return to chamber faster than you fired. The worst thing that could happen to you would be to have an attacker grab your hands. If you "hang technique" (leave the strike on target) in practice, you will endanger yourself in a real self-defense situation. (See "Breaking bad habits" in chapter four.)

Working with a Partner

Working with a partner is ideal training and will help you to understand and perfect your strikes. *Work only in slow motion when practicing with another to avoid accidents.*

Use a right palm heel to center of face.

28

ABOVE:
Continue with left
palm heel to solar plexus.
(Notice fingers to the side.)

RIGHT:
A right palm heel to the groin.
(Notice fingers pointed down.)

1. *Face each other in shoulder-width stances.* Get as close as an attacker would come. The first person to work should use the right, then the left, hand. Go up and down the body with well-placed palm heel techniques on the allowed striking areas. (Refer to the palm heel striking chart.) Don't forget shove shock.

For instance, if you're starting at the top of the body, use a right palm heel to the center of the face, continue with a left palm heel to the solar plexus. Then you might use two palm heels to the ribs, then another right or left palm heel to the groin. Use continuous motion.

29

Even though you are working in super-slow motion, actually touch the palm heel to the area you are aiming at, then return to chamber. *Do not stop short of your target in practice, or you will do the same if attacked.* Program yourself correctly. As long as you work extremely slowly there will be no injuries to you or your partner.

2. *Turn your target partner around.* Now go up and down your partner's body from the back. Still working in very slow motion, use alternate hands, then use both at the same time to go for the target areas on the back. The back of the neck is an easy target and a paralyzing strike. (Make sure you strike below the skull bone and not on it.) Two palm heels directed to the kidneys are devastating!

*Palm heel
strike to
side of
face.*

3. *Turn your target partner to the side.* Again use your palm heels slowly and wisely. Aim for the side of the face, then the ribs. Go for these vulnerable areas with a plan: make sure your strikes are accurate; make sure only the palm heel touches the target area; make sure you come right back to chamber; use alternate hands.

4. *Now it's your turn to be the target.* Repeat the whole procedure. Working slowly, practice palm heel strikes to the front, back, and side. Make this a real workout. Alternate back and forth ten times each. This is valuable work time—you are programming your computer.

To strengthen your palm heel strikes even more, do push-ups placing most of your weight on the palm heels as opposed to spreading it over the entire surface of the palm. This exercise will also give you a feeling of contact and toughen up your palm heels.

30

BLOCKING

It is best to work with a partner for this drill. If you haven't got someone to work with you will have to imagine the punches coming at you. It will be more difficult, but nothing is impossible. Exercise total concentration, and you will learn. *Partners should work in shoulder-width stances very close to each other.* This is an in-close blocking drill. When someone tries to strike you, he comes very close. That's what you're going to learn to deal with. Both hands always move at the same time.

High Block

1. *Face each other, shoulder-width stances, hands relaxed at sides.*

High block, low strike.

2. *Striking partner goes for your head with right fist in slow motion.* This can be an overhead punch or a punch straight to the face. Either way this block will work.

3. *Bring your left arm across your body and up to block; strike with right palm heel to attacker's low stomach.* Make sure you turn the soft part of your forearm up to catch the blow. You don't want to make contact with the bony part. *Both of your hands move at exactly the same time.* Return hands to relaxed position at your sides.

31

4. *Striking partner goes for your head with left fist in slow motion. Block with your right arm; strike with your left palm heel to attacker's low stomach.*[2]
Repeat twenty times, alternating sides.

Move toward your attacker as you strike, trying to get out of the way of the approaching blow. I know you haven't had to move out of the way of punches, and this is requiring you to move everything at once. Just keep working in slow motion.

Middle Block

1. *Face each other in shoulder-width stances. Hands relaxed at sides.*
2. *Striking partner attacks with slow motion right fist punch to stomach.*

Middle block and strike.

3. *Your left hand crosses your middle to block, as your right hand strikes into the solar plexus.*[3]
4. *Striking partner alternates and punches with slow motion left fist to stomach. You block with right hand; strike with left.*
Repeat twenty times, alternating sides. Remember, both hands move at the same time.

---

[2]You may also strike to the solar plexus with your palm heel. This is a breathing system strike, but don't go any higher than the solar plexus. A rule of thumb for blocking is: high block—low strike; low strike—high block.

[3]Heavy winter clothing would cushion this palm heel strike to the solar plexus. A leather jacket would absorb enough of the blow to make it ineffective. If an attacker were heavily padded, you would therefore substitute a knee to groin, heel to knee, or heel to shin strike along with the middle block.

Low Block

1. *Face each other in shoulder-width stances. Hands relaxed at sides.*
2. *Striking partner attacks with slow motion right fist to groin.*

Low block, high strike.

3. *Your left palm heel slaps down to deflect (change the path of) the punch, as your right palm heel strikes to attacker's center face.*[4]

4. *Striking partner alternates sides and attacks with left punch. You block with right arm deflecting palm heel and strike with left palm heel to attacker's center face at the same time.*

Work on these simple blocks a lot. Practice them until they are spontaneous, then try to get some expert martial art supervision for advanced blocking.

When you work on blocking with a partner, make sure your partner really tries to strike you. Work very, very slowly at first. As you become familiar with the blocking system, put on a little speed. Gradually increase the speed. If you don't do this you are fooling yourself. An attacker on the street is not going to move in slow motion. He's going to try to knock you out! So, if you are going to bother to learn to block, don't fool around. Once you understand the mechanics of the techniques, go for real! If you miss a block and get hit, that's good for you. It will make you more aware of the realities, build quicker blocking reflexes. After you have been practicing a while, you will naturally start shifting your body into the strike and away from the oncoming punch.

You can work blindfolded to make yourself more aware and better at blocking. Both you and your partner should put on blindfolds and work slowly

---

[4]You may also practice striking into the solar plexus with the low block.

at first, then increase your speed. This will teach you many things and bring your awareness level to a high peak.

When it's your turn to attack, really try to strike your partner, slowly at first, but then laying on some steam. That is the only way two people can do valid blocking work. That is why it's good to work on blocks with a man. He's going to be aggressive and force you to stop him. That's good training for you.

Here's an old martial art blocking story for you to think about:

There was a young man who wanted to study with a wonderful martial art master. The young man went to the master and requested instruction. The master told him he would have to serve as a kitchen slave in order to pay. The young man agreed and moved into the master's house.

The first morning, the young man was sweeping the kitchen floor. The master came in and beat him soundly with a stick. Every day thereafter the master came into the kitchen and beat the disciple.

At the end of a year the young man went to the master and humbly begged to know when his training would begin. The master called forth his best students and told them one by one to fight the kitchen boy. With all their practiced techniques, not one of them could even touch him. The kitchen boy had become a blocking expert of the highest order; avoiding the master's daily blows had taught him well. He was given a place among the students. That same boy went on to become the best swordsman in all of feudal Japan.

I don't expect you to check into a master's kitchen and be beaten daily. But I think you should subject yourself to blocking stress whenever possible. So go ahead, pick yourself a tough, aggressive partner for blocking drills.

34   This particular blocking drill is different from most beginning blocking systems, because I am teaching you to block and strike at the same time. Most systems teach block *then* strike. By moving both your hands at the same time, you are taking an advantage, and this gives you another trick up your sleeve.

Let's take a logical look at blocking. It takes a tremendous amount of practice to block a full-speed attack effectively. You are working at the basic beginnings only. I cannot take you further in this book and in good conscience expect you to protect yourself. Further blocking would require far more complicated work. I would want to supervise you personally in my class.

Here's a blocking motto for you: *YOU MOVE; I MOVE FIRST.*

Think of blocking a blow this way: if someone tries to strike you, it just means he gets hit.

HEEL STRIKING

To be practiced in shoulder-width stance, hands up[5] in guard position as in the photos.

1. *Pull your right leg to the chamber position as pictured.* Make sure your *knee is above your waist.* Pull your heel back toward your groin. Tighten your toes and pull them back. Your right arm should be forward. This is the chamber position for all kicks. *Your left leg,* the leg on which you stand, *must be flexed at the knee.*

2. *Look at the right side at knee level. Extend your right heel.* Keep the toes pulled back. Stay low on the standing leg. Keep the top of your body still; do

---

[5]If the right leg is working, the right arm should be forward. If the left leg is working, the left arm is forward. This is a protective measure and prepares you for blocking and striking with your lead hand.

not lean away from the kick. Stay centered and balanced working in slow motion.

3. *Return to chamber position.*

4. *Lower your right leg and return to the flexed knee, shoulder-width stance.*

5. *Alternate sides, look to the left at knee height. Kick to the left at knee height.*

Repeat fifty times in slow motion. Work for smooth, fluid movement. *Do not* bob up and down as you change legs and hands. Keep your knees well bent all the time you are working on this technique, never straighten up. Keep your body at one low level, grip the earth with your toes.

Repeat fifty times at full speed, with a yell of spirit. Pop that heel out. Here's a kicking rule: if the heel goes out at 50 miles-per-hour, it returns to chamber at 100 miles-per-hour.

Working with a Partner

1. *Your partner should stand close to you, facing your left side* and a bit to the rear. Look at the knee nearest you.

2. *Chamber your left leg, then extend the left heel* and lightly touch your target—the knee nearest you. Fully extend your heel toward the ground; if it slides down your partner's shin, all the better. (See side grab combination in chapter five for practical application of kick to knee and down the shin to arch of foot.)

3. *Return the kicking leg to chamber; then return to shoulder-width stance.*

4. *Turn around so your partner is on your right side. Repeat.*
Repeat twenty times, alternating sides.

Using this technique, you can kick the front of the knee as in the photos here, or you can kick the side of the knee. Either way this is a knee-breaking technique.

LEG CHECKING WITH THE HEEL

To be practiced in shoulder-width stance, hands up in guard position.

1. *Raise your right leg to the chamber position. Invert your heel.* Pull your toes back. Right arm should be forward since right leg is working. Make sure your standing leg is flexed and toes are gripping the ground.

2. *Extend your heel fully down your front center line. The heel stays inverted and extends beyond your toes. The toes remain pulled back.* Only your heel will make contact with the target   37

3.   *Return to chamber.*
4.   *Return to shoulder-width stance.*
5.   *Alternate to left leg, bringing left hand forward.*
Repeat fifty times in slow motion.
Repeat fifty times at full speed with a yell of spirit.

Working with a Partner
1.   *Face your partner, arms up in guard position.*

2.   *Alternate right then left leg checks to top of knees.* Work carefully as this is a dangerous kick, and the knee is easily damaged. If you were to fully extend your leg at full speed, the knee would break. If you contact above the knee, you still have tremendous stopping power. This is truly a leg check.

The higher your chamber is, the more stopping power your leg check will have. An attacker running at you full speed would be devastated by this leg check.

Make sure you see your striking point.

Repeat twenty times in slow motion. Change hands as you alternate legs. Stay low in your stance—balance is very important. If your stance is not firm, your leg check will lose power.

STOMPING
By learning to strike with your heels, you have also learned how to stomp. The only difference is that your stomping target is on the ground.

38

*Practicing
groin stomping.*

*Practicing
face stomping.*

Working with a Partner

Have your partner lie down on the floor, face up. Stand over your partner, and in very slow motion, do your heel strike. Practice aiming your heel to the face, stomach, and groin.

Stay well bent at the knee so that you are solidly balanced. Stay close to your striking point; don't try to reach it from far away. Have your partner turn over, face down, and practice your stomps to the back of the body. Practice with both your right and left heels.

If you don't have a partner to work with, imagine an attacker lying beneath you, and practice-stomp. This is an ideal technique to use if you have temporarily stunned an opponent with a breathing system blow, an elbow strike, etc., but have not knocked him out or hurt him enough for you to escape easily.

Stomping to the face and throat may cause death.

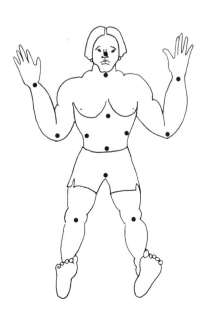

*Stomping Chart
(Front View)*

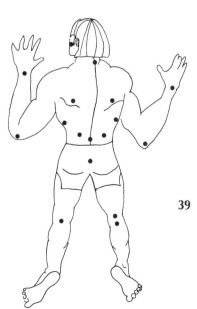

*Stomping Chart
(Back View)*

39

FALLING TO THE GROUND AND STRIKING WITH THE HEELS

By learning these heel kicks, you have also learned to defend yourself from the ground. In many cases women get knocked down and find themselves on the ground with an attacker coming toward them. *This is a position of advantage for you. In order for your attacker to reach you, he must move his legs into your heel striking range.*

Fall in the chambered position.

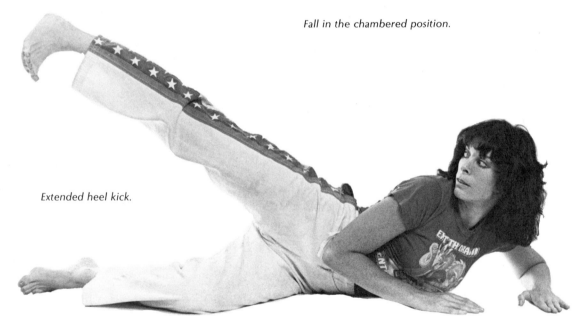

Extended heel kick.

Practice falling to the ground slowly, breaking your fall with your palm heels and the soft part of your forearms. *Land in a leg-chambered position.* Do this on both your right and left sides.

Repeat twenty times, alternating sides.

Remember, if you are knocked down, it may mean contacting cement. Knowing how to break a fall is important. Make sure your bones do not touch the ground—only the soft parts of your body. You may sustain bruises in this way, but that's a lot better than broken bones.

40

*Working
with a partner
on ground fighting.*

Working with a Partner

Have your partner give you a slight push. Fall to the ground in a chambered position keeping your eyes directly on your partner's knees. Have your partner slowly approach you. Strike the knee nearest you as soon as it comes into range *at least twice.* This means returning to chamber, then heel striking again. Work in very slow motion so that you do not injure your partner.

Repeat twenty times in slow motion, alternating sides. Feel your hip behind the kick.

Working by Yourself

Now you understand what you are doing and where you are kicking. *Work again by yourself—this time execute two full-speed kicks from the ground; then get to your feet as quickly as possible, prepared to run.* You and your partner may do this side by side. See who is faster. Which one of you can fall to the ground, complete two kicks, and get to your feet first? Use your yell of spirit. Whose yell is louder? Whose is more terrifying? Make sure the kick is slightly to the rear, so that your hip is behind the heel. Think of your buttocks producing the power for the heel strike.

I have developed this particular type of falling to the ground for my students so they will never be caught off-guard. I have heard over and over again from women who were assaulted: "I never saw him; I just felt a blow and was knocked to the ground, then he came." Regardless of whether his intention was to rape, to further assault, or to rob, the attacker always approached *after* knocking the victim down.

You are strong on the ground. You have a total body grip on mother earth. This is better than just being able to grip with your toes. You have good back- **41** up for your heel strike. The attacker has the disadvantage of having to put his knees forward. *Once you knock out his suspension system, he cannot come after you.* Knees are so delicate; ask any athlete. If you miss the knee and strike the shinbone, your heel kick will be just as effective. You are still attacking his suspension system. Kick with all your might: hard, hard; fast, fast.

If you are knocked to the ground, you must fall into this chambered position. But *make your attacker think you are scared.* Do not telegraph the fact that you are going to strike. Your attacker will assume you are drawing up in fear. That's good. Let him believe he has an easy mark. This will make it even more simple for you to catch him off guard. In this situation, I would recommend pleading as he approaches—something like, "Please don't hurt me." Then strike with deadly accuracy the *second* his forward leg comes close.

This is very important work. Practice falling in all sorts of positions. Have your partner knock you down in slow motion from the rear. Watch how you land; see what variations you can come up with. If you raise your heel higher, you can even strike his groin. There are many possibilities; the more you practice, the more capable you will be of variations. Just remember, the first order is to protect yourself. Land lightly, like a cat; ready to spring.

*You can also
strike the groin
from this ground position.*

Wonder Woman School, FOUR
Part II:
Basic Techniques

FINGER JABBING TO THE EYES AND THE THROAT

The leading finger jab is the longest of all hand weapons as well as the fastest because of the little force needed. Like a cobra, your finger jab should be felt and not seen.—Bruce Lee, Tao of Jeet Kune Do

We must discuss finger jabbing to the eyes, the technique you are about to learn, before we proceed further. This is an extremely lethal technique. It may cause death and should be used *only* to save your life! The last-minute turning over of the strike (when the elbow passes the rib cage) causes a snapping, corkscrew motion that can destroy the eye. Since the finger jab moves on an upward path, it enters the eye from the bottom. This may cause the eye to leave the socket. Shock will probably occur; death may follow. The least that would happen from delivering this finger jab would be an uncontrollable watering of the eyes, accompanied by intense pain.

Due to the fact that you use "shocking flickering force" rather than punching force, the finger jab also is like swatting a fly. Accuracy is what counts. Choose your target during movement and let go to recover with ready reinforcements.—Bruce Lee

Close your eye. Tap the closed lid with your own finger. Feel how disturbing it is—the eye is so sensitive. Imagine a full-speed thrust to your eye with a pointed weapon (your finger jab). *There is nothing an attacker can do after receiving such a thrust except grab his eyes and try to alleviate the pain.*

Beware of the exception: the attacker under the influence of a heavy drug. Alcohol or narcotics can have enough of a pain-deadening effect to make an attacker numb. You will know how to deal with such an attacker after reading chapter seven.

Occasionally women leave my classes after this technique is explained. They **43** tell me frankly that they cannot deal with the concept of taking out someone's eye. My answer is: fine, then deal with the concept of your own death.

Even I was squeamish about the thought of the eye jab. Then I had occasion to counsel and teach self-defense to a woman who had been raped and badly knifed by an attacker. After listening to the gory details of her nightmarish experience, I was glad to have a strong technique like finger jabbing in my repertoire.

> *The leading finger jab is one of the most efficient weapons, especially in self-defense, and should be cultivated to the highest form of proficiency.* —Bruce Lee

You may never in your life have to call on such a technique. But learn it, and know it well!

A full, thrusting, finger jab to the windpipe is a knockout strike and considered very dangerous. If delivered with enough focus (to the back of the skull), death may result.

Finger jabbing to the throat may also be used as a control tactic. (See chapter ten.)

FINGER JABBING TO THE EYES (AND THROAT)

Use a shoulder-width stance. Flex both knees. Grip with the toes.

1. *Begin with both hands chambered, middle finger crossed over the index finger.* Make sure the two extended fingers are pressed well against each other for support. Check to see that you have formed one sharp point with the two fingers. Keep them pointed toward your center line, ready to strike.

2. *Move your right finger weapon forward, toward center body.* Keep the edge of your palm hard against your rib cage, then the edge of your wrist, then the forearm. Your finger weapon should now be directly in front of your solar plexus (on the center line of your body), tipped slightly upward. Keep moving your arm forward. Now your elbow should be pressed hard against your rib cage. *As the elbow passes the rib cage your hand must turn over.* Keep going forward until the strike is fully extended. Keep a small flex in the elbow. Make sure your finger weapon is centered and aimed slightly upwards.

3. *Alternate hands.* As the left finger weapon starts moving slowly forward, seeking the center line of your body, the right will move slowly backward. Both hands will stay close to the rib cage. Both hands must turn at the same time, resulting in an extended left finger jab (with flexed elbow) and the right finger weapon returned to the chamber position. *Stay on that center line.*

Repeat fifty times in slow motion. Work for the flowing-like-water motion that carries your strike smoothly to its target. Flex your knees deeply, and sink into your stance. Keep your shoulders back. Only your fingers and arm should move forward—concentrate on that and the center-line path to your target, developed by pressing against your rib cage all the time.

Repeat fifty times at full speed, using a loud yell of spirit with each strike.

The power for this strike comes from your hips and feet. Your grip on the earth is power; think of yourself as part of the earth. Grip with your toes. Keep your shoulders back. Sink deeper into your stance. Most important of all, center your finger jabs.

Besides being a deadly weapon, this technique will develop your aim and give you a good chance to use your upper body. (You will notice a firming of the upper arms and chest, a general strengthening of the top body, and better posture.) This exercise is particularly valuable as it develops and trains the eyes.   **45**

Working with a Partner

You need to be more careful with this technique than with any other I will teach you. *You must move in super-slow motion only!*

1. Face each other in the shoulder-width stance. Get close to each other—this is a close-in technique. Your target partner should have closed eyes. Slowly, slowly *bring your finger jab forward. Gently touch the bottom of the eye nearest you.* Never cross over to the other eye. In an emergency situation, you might strike the nose bone. Remember, the shortest path is always a straight line. *Make sure you actually touch your target.* Don't practice stopping short of your target, or you do it when attacked. Work slowly, be relaxed, and there should be no injuries. It is important that you seek and find your target with your finger weapon.

2. *Use alternate hands.* Make sure you are well-flexed at your knees. Sink down in your stance—your strike should be moving on an upward path to its eye target.

Repeat twenty times with each hand.

3. *Repeat the same technique to the windpipe.* Again, make sure you actually contact your target lightly. The throat gives you a larger area to strike; just be careful not to hit the top of the chest bone.

In slow motion repeat ten times with each hand.

Finger jabbing to the throat

The Moving Rings

This moving ring exercise will develop an accurate, fast strike and keen eyesight.—Master Thomas Agero

1. *Make a ring with your thumb and forefinger.* Hold that finger ring in front of you at eye level. Have your partner stand in front of you, as one would on the street (not in a chambered hand position), and finger jab through that circle with right, then left, finger jabs. Work slowly; work for accuracy.

2. *Slowly move the finger ring back and forth in front of you.* Your partner must strike into the moving circle with alternate hands.

Repeat twenty times in slow motion.

Repeat ten times at full speed with the yell of spirit.

3. *Make two finger rings.* Have your partner strike with both hands at the same time.

Repeat twenty times in slow motion.

4. *Move the two rings back and forth at a faster pace.* Your partner must work for accuracy.

Repeat ten times at full speed with full yell of spirit.

Now it's your turn: repeat the above instructions.

ELBOW STRIKING

All elbow strikes are to be practiced in a shoulder-width stance.

Elbow Strike to the Head

1. *Begin with both hands in closed-fist position.* (To make a fist roll your fingers up tightly and hold them all together with your thumb.)

2. *Reach forward with your left hand open.* Make sure your left hand (the grabbing hand) is centered in front of your solar plexus.

48

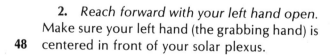

3. *Throw your right elbow into your out-stretched left hand. Do not* bring the hand to the elbow; bring the elbow to the hand. Make a hitting sound with the elbow, slapping it into the palm. Make sure that your elbow and hand are centered on your power line.

4. *Return your elbow to the chamber position.* Leave your grabbing hand out.

Repeat twenty-five times in slow motion. Alternate sides and repeat another twenty-five times, moving slowly. Your elbow should make a sound as it hits your palm.

Imagine that your grabbing hand is holding the back of an attacker's head. Your forward-moving elbow will be meeting that hand through the attacker's face.

Do twenty-five full-speed strikes on each side with a yell of spirit.

Elbow Strike to the Rear
1. *Begin with both hands in closed-fist, chamber position.*

2. *Reach forward with both hands as though to grab handles. Center your hands.*

3. *Think of grabbing two handles and pulling them back to chamber position. Make sure your elbows are directly behind your hands,* not stuck out like birds wings.

This is an important technique to know if you are attacked from behind. (See chapter five, back grab combination.) The elbow smashes into an attacker's breathing system. In order to have enough power to execute this blow fully, you must train yourself to return all the way to the chamber position. So be sure your fists return to your ribcage.

Repeat twenty-five times in slow motion.

Repeat twenty-five times at full speed with yell of spirit.

Elbow Strike Downward

1. *Begin with both fists closed in chamber position.*

2. *Reach straight up with your right hand, palm facing out, as if reaching for an overhead handle.* Keep your hand centered.

3. Grab the handle, turning hand toward you, and pull down. Keep elbow pointed slightly *toward your left side.*

4. *Reach up and repeat.*
Repeat twenty-five times with each elbow, in slow motion.
Repeat twenty-five times, at full speed, with loud yell of spirit.
This strike can be used to deliver a downward blow to chest, stomach, or back.

Elbow Strike Upward
1. *Begin with both fists closed in chamber position.*

2. *Bring your right elbow up past your head. Your fist should be alongside your right ear, the palm facing the ear.*

3. *Return to chamber position.*
4. *Repeat with your left elbow.*
Practice twenty-five strikes on each elbow in slow motion.
Practice twenty-five strikes on each elbow at full speed with a loud yell of spirit.

The upward-rising elbow is used to strike under an attacker's chin. Since the chin is a small target area, be sure your elbow stays on the center line of your body. That way, your strike will always be on target.

Elbow Strike to the Side
1. *Begin with both fists closed in chamber position.*

2. *With your right hand, reach for an imaginary handle, as far across your body as possible. Eyes must look to the right at the approaching opponent.*

3. *Pull the handle on a straight line as far as you can.*

52

4. *Reach across your body again and repeat.*
Repeat twenty-five times on each side in slow motion.
Repeat twenty-five times at full speed with a loud yell of spirit.

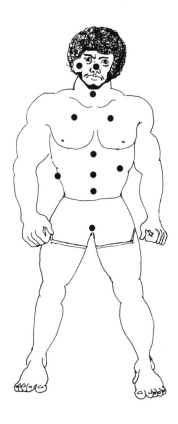

Elbow Strike Chart (Front View)

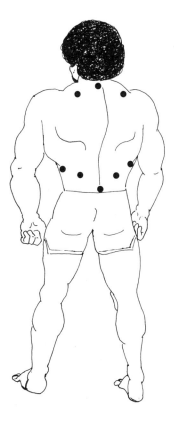

Elbow Strike Chart (Back View)

If an attacker were approaching you from the side, this strike could be aimed at the throat, the solar plexus, or the face (depending on attacker's height), and if you were knocked to the ground, you could use it to hit the groin.

Working with a Partner

Your elbows are about the best natural weapons on your body for close-in fighting. With some practice you can learn to whip them around in amazingly effective patterns. Your elbows are strong, and you will feel no pain when you make contact with them.

The most important thing about elbow fighting is to smash each strike all the way through. This means paying strict attention to each detail as you practice.

Make sure you see what you are going to strike. If you can see it, you can hit it.

Elbow Strike to the Head

1. *Face each other in shoulder-width stances.*
2. *Reach forward and grab your partner by the back of the head.*

3. *Slowly bring your elbow to your partner's face. Actually touch the center of your partner's face with your elbow. Be careful. See his or her face.*

Repeat ten times with each elbow.

Elbow Strike to the Rear

1. *Have your partner stand directly behind,* and close to you, as an attacker would stand.

2. *Dip your hip away to expose your partner's breathing system; strike slowly, and touch the solar plexus with your elbow.* It is important that you always try to see the spot you are striking. Moving your hip aside is of vital importance and will assure your contacting the solar plexus or, if the attacker is very tall, the vulnerable lower stomach area. *So move your hip on each practice strike.*

Repeat ten times with each elbow.

Elbow Striking Downward

1. *Face your partner in a shoulder-width stance.*

2. *In slow motion, elbow strike downward into stomach.*
Repeat ten times with each arm.

1. *Have your partner* (still in shoulder-width stance) *bend backwards as though falling.*

2. *In slow motion, elbow strike downward into stomach. Repeat ten times with each arm.*

1. *Have your partner bend over in a forward position.*
2. *Strike to back of neck with slow downward elbow.*
Repeat ten times with each arm.

1. *Have your partner bend over again.*

2. *Strike to kidney and base of spine with slow downward elbow strike.*

Repeat kidney strike ten times, repeat strike to base of spine ten times, both in slow motion.   **55**

Elbow Striking Upward
1. *Face your partner in shoulder-width stance.*

2. *Contact under the chin in very slow motion.*

Repeat ten times with each arm.

Elbow Striking to the Side
1. *Have your partner stand at a right angle to you.*

2. *Place your elbow strike directly in the center of partner's body. Depending on the height of your partner, you may contact the throat, solar plexus, or face. Use slow motion only.*

Repeat ten times with each arm.

56

KNEE STRIKING

Knee striking must be practiced in a shoulder-width stance. Make sure your knees are flexed, toes digging into the earth.

1. *Lift your right knee as high as you can*—try to reach your right shoulder. *At the same time, bring your hands up in a defensive position.*[1] Since your right knee is forward, your right hand will be the lead *(front)* hand. *Don't bend your body toward the rising knee.* The knee must come up. This movement is accomplished with the stomach and thigh muscles. Think about that as you pull your knee *high! Make sure the leg you are standing on remains flexed at the knee* as you pull the right knee strike high.

2. *Return your right foot to the floor, resuming your shoulder-width stance.* Make sure both knees are flexed.

3. *Lift your left knee as high as you can* —try to reach your left shoulder. *At the same time, your left hand will come forward as the lead hand.* Remember, don't bend your body; only raise the knee. Your other leg stays flexed.

4. *Alternate knees, hands always co-ordinating* (left leg up, left hand leading; right leg up, right hand leading). Make sure your standing leg remains flexed.[2]

Repeat fifty times in slow, flowing motion. Work for balance. Practice body stillness. Keep your foot under your knee, pulled tight toward your body. Don't let your foot stick out. Check your form. Get the feel of the strike.

Repeat fifty times at full speed, screaming with each strike. Pay attention to your yell of spirit. Would it scare you? Make your scream for real! Now is the time to sweat.

---

[1]When actually applying a knee strike, your hands would be gripping an attacker: by the head for a head strike, by the shoulders for a groin strike, etc. But for practice, since you don't have an attacker to work with, just raise your hands. It's always a good idea to get used to throwing your hands up. In that way, you are ready to strike and use your blocking system; ready to protect yourself at all times.

[2]A flexed knee is a safety measure. A straightened leg receiving a blow to the knee will break. If the knee is bent and gets hit, injury will still occur, but it is not likely to break. The same principle applies to the elbows.

The knee is a nature-given weapon, strong and simple to employ. Used effectively, your knees will always protect you. (For photos of Sensi [Instructor] Filson executing knee strikes to the face and groin, see chapter five.)

Knee Strike to the Groin

To execute properly a strike to the groin with a rising knee, *you must be very close to your attacker. Your knee must be deep between the attacker's legs,* then rise *all* the way up, exactly the way you practiced. Do not stop upon feeling contact, that's not good enough. *Your striking point is the middle of the stomach.* How do you get there? *Up through* the pelvic structure!

Knee Strike to the Face

In order to use a knee strike to the face, *you will have to grab the attacker's head and pull it down as you bring your knee strike up. Your striking point is the back of the head.* How do you get there? *Through* the face! *Double knee strikes are easy.* As soon as your first strike contacts its target, return quickly to shoulder-width stance and bring your other knee up through the face, exactly the way you practiced.

The knee strike to the face is to be used only when your life is threatened. This strike is very powerful and causes so much damage to the face (broken nose, teeth, and cheekbones) that it may result in your attacker's death. At least he will require hospitalization.

All advantage is on your side when you use the knee strike to the face. You have his head firmly gripped in your hands (you may grab his hair if it's long and offers a good hold) so it's easy to direct the strike and achieve maximum focus. Since you train to deliver two strikes, one after the other, you're dealing double trouble.

After practicing this strike for a while with a partner, you will come to see a clear path open to the head giving you a chance to use this strike.

Knee Strike to the Spine

To strike the spine with a rising knee, simply *grab the head and pull the attacker backward and down* as you bring your knee up. *Your striking point is*

LEFT: Spine strike from the side.

RIGHT: Spine strike from the back.

the stomach. How do you get there? Up through the spine. You may be either directly in back of an attacker or at his side. When an emergency situation takes place, you never know what's going to happen or which way you will have to strike. You will not always be face to face with your assailant. For instance, an attacker might try to punch you. You might step out of the way to avoid being hit and find yourself in a perfect position to use a knee to the spine. There is no rhyme or reason to a sudden confrontation and you must be prepared to defend yourself from all vantage points.

Strike to the stomach with the knee.

Knee Strike to the Stomach

To strike into the stomach with the rising knee, you may stand to the front of the attacker, *grip his shoulders, and pull his body toward you as you raise your knee high to strike. The striking point is the spine and you get there through the stomach.* This strike sometimes occurs by accident. You may intend to throw a knee strike to the groin; your attacker may make a sudden move that causes your strike to contact the stomach area instead. That's all right; your attacker will still be stunned. Since you have delivered a breathing-system strike, he may be knocked out.

THE "MONKEY KNEE"

The "monkey knee" fascinates me, both because of its versatility and its origin—which goes back to China in 1842 during the rule of the hated Ch'ing dynasty.[3]

[3]David Chow and Richard Spangler, *Kung Fu: History, Philosophy and Technique* (Doubleday).

Kau See was a man of the people, well-known for his ground-fighting abilities. His reputation spread, and a conscription officer came to draft him into the army. The fighter refused. The induction officer tried to take him by force to Manchu military headquarters. A fight ensued. The officer was killed, and the offender was jailed in the Bamboo Forest of China.

Kau See served an eight-year sentence surrounded by monkeys and apes. The Chinese penal authorities used apes as watchdogs.[4] There were families of monkeys living in the trees and Kau See observed their conflicts with other apes or predators. He watched, and he practiced.

Thus was born the "monkey system" of fighting. There was the "timid monkey," the "angry monkey," the "rock monkey," etc. The most interesting of all was the "drunken monkey." Kau See had watched an ape gulp down some forgotten wine, get roaring drunk, and then start screaming and making erratic, frantic movements. Other monkeys ganged up on him. But even in his inebriated state, the wobbling monkey was able to defend himself. The prisoner realized the effectiveness of lulling an opponent into overconfidence by appearing drunk, then delivering full-force head and groin kicks.

The enterprising prisoner also observed forty ways to fight with a stick, from his jungle instructors. When Kau See was released from prison he taught his style of fighting and became known as the "Monkey Master."

An instructor of mine recently returned from Hong Kong, where he had studied the monkey styles. He displayed the theatrical and devastating drunken monkey style by going into a seemingly spastic display, jerking about in a crazy pattern. His opponent was mesmerized by the weird movements and caught totally off-guard when my teacher scored three lightning-quick, perfectly-placed techniques.

My instructor taught me the monkey knee. It is always effective and sneaky. You should have it in your bag of tricks. Being able to direct your knee in this unusual way is a great advantage. It is a rare person who has seen this type of knee striking. An attacker would probably not be on guard against a well-delivered monkey knee.

The monkey knee serves as a great middle-of-the body strike to the ribs and to the stomach and back (spine). Like your other knee strikes, the monkey knee comes from a shoulder-width stance. The only difference is that instead of rising straight up, the monkey knee requires you to tip, swivel, or pivot your hip in order to send the knee on its circular path to target. This strike is best learned when working with a partner, *so I will expect you to learn from the partner photos.*

If you are caught on the ground next to an attacker, you may use a monkey knee to the nearest vulnerable point. You may also use this technique to the *face, stomach, ribs, or groin* if the attacker is *face-up.* If he falls in a face-down position, you may use the monkey knee to his *spine, ribs,* or *kidneys.* This would be a totally logical yet unexpected move on your part.

---

[4]If a prisoner broke out, the monkeys would make a loud chattering noise to alert Chinese army guards.

Groin strike with rising knee. Make sure you are very close to each other. (It is advisable for a male partner to wear an athletic protector.) Work very slowly. Make sure your knee is deep between your partner's legs. Grip your partner's shoulders. Raise the knee all the way up. Since you are not really striking it will come out of the partner's legs, but draw it up to your partner's waist level outside the leg opening anyway. This will train you always to raise your knee all the way.

Repeat twenty times in slow motion using alternate knees.

Face strike with rising knee. Practicing this strike requires extreme caution. Grab your partner's head slowly, and carefully. Make sure you have a good grip. Bring the head down and your knee up, slowly. Now, take a small, slow hop as you change legs and bring the other knee up slowly to the face that is still pulled down. Remember, these double knee strikes to the face are devastating. Be careful not to hurt each other in practice!

Repeat twenty times in slow motion.

61

Stomach (solar plexus) strike with rising knee. Grab your partner's shoulders, slowly pulling the body toward you as you raise your knee.

Repeat twenty times in slow motion.

Spine strike with rising knee. Grab your partner's hair, or head, from the rear, bend the body slowly backward and strike with rising knee.

Repeat twenty times in slow motion.

Monkey knee strikes to the stomach (solar plexus), groin, and front ribs. (Your target will depend on the height of your partner and the opening available.)

Face each other in shoulder-width stances. Notice in the picture that my student is executing a monkey knee to the low stomach. If she were to bend the leg she's standing on, the strike would go to her partner's groin. Note also the shoulder grip.

Practice twenty slow motion monkey knees. Try to vary your striking points (groin, low stomach, and [if you can reach that high], the low ribs).

Monkey knee strike to the back (spine, low ribs, kidneys). *Position yourself behind your partner, and work as illustrated in photo.* Again, try to vary your striking points according to body positioning and height of your partner.

Monkey knee strike from the ground. Have your partner lie on the ground as pictured and start with the face strike my student is executing here. Put yourself in different positions on the floor so you are close to different parts of your partner's body, and practice ground monkey knees to all vulnerable areas. This is very important work and may come in handy, so pay strict attention to being able to strike from the floor. Work slowly but accurately.

With partner lying face up repeat ten times each to the: face; low stomach; solar plexus; low ribs and groin.

With partner lying face down repeat ten times each to the: spine; kidneys; and low ribs.

During this valuable workout, try lying a small distance away from your partner so that you have to *scramble across the floor to get to your striking point.* This is good practice and will help set you up to deal with any situation.

BREAKING BAD HABITS

It is easy to develop bad habits. It is important to break a bad habit the minute you find out it exists. Do not wait and tell yourself you'll fix it up during your next workout. Stop whatever you're working on and break the bad habit. Here are some common errors which you might find you've picked up:

"Hanging Technique"

The term "hanging technique" means leaving a strike on its target. For instance, if you throw a palm heel strike to the center of an attacker's face and leave it there for one millimeter of a second too long, the attacker will surely grab your hand and have you. The same applies to a kick left "out there" too long.

It is therefore of major importance to your safety that you return all techniques to chamber much faster than they go out to target.

If you sense during workout periods that you are hanging technique, concentrate on stopping it immediately! Working with a partner is the time when hanging technique really shows up. So make sure you and your partner check each other out.

Favoring One Side

It is normal to have a stronger or more developed side. The right-handed person has more natural dexterity for right-handed techniques. It is important that you develop both sides of your body evenly. If you catch one side performing less perfectly than the other, stop your normal workout and work only on your weaker side for a couple of days. Then go back to a two-sided workout, but double the work on your weaker side for another two days. If one side is still less dexterous, start all over. Go for perfection. What if you are right-handed, defending yourself from harm, and your right hand gets broken? Does that mean you can't survive because you can fight and block with only one side? Not you—your *whole body* must function for you with balance and symmetry.

Stargazing

If you let your eyes wander when you are working by yourself, you will have a problem when it comes time to hit a target. *See your target in your mind's eye.* Stay focused. Stay clear in your mind about what you are doing and what part of your opponent's body you are contacting all the time you are training. Always assume your opponent is directly in front of you, and keep your eyes centered just as your technique should be.

Adjusting Clothing

This is an easy habit to acquire and one that can get you hurt. That moment's hesitation to adjust your clothing before striking will lose you the advantage of surprise. Most people don't realize that they have picked up this very bad habit.

Sticking Out Your Tongue in Concentration

This is another bad habit that can hurt you badly. In an emergency situation you might clamp your teeth down and bite off your own tongue. I have seen this happen at tournaments. Keep your tongue in your mouth.

FIVE

Wonder Woman School, FIVE
Part III:
Empty-Hand
Combinations

Now that you've learned basic hand and foot techniques, you're ready to string them together into combinations for practical self-defense.[1] *One never uses a lone technique for self-protection.* The well-trained woman strikes swiftly using a variety of techniques that are confusing and painful to an adversary.

The three combinations described in this chapter are simple and effective. *Never use movements more complex* than necessary. You already know how to execute all of these kicks and strikes (and many more). Now you must learn to apply them rationally to an actual situation. *The only way you can program yourself to reflexively defend with these combinations is to practice them thousands of times.*

Each of these combinations has many variables. Once you know a pattern well you will be able to make necessary changes spontaneously. You will have to. In an emergency situation, physical violence is the name of the game, and nothing is predictable.

It is always best to work on combinations with a partner. If this is not possible, work in the air and imagine an attacker. Pay close attention to the photos here. Notice the exact striking-points; see the other openings available; think about all the other techniques you know and how they could be applied to the same situation.

You will be working at two speeds: slow motion and full speed. Use your slow motion time wisely and achieve 100 percent perfect form. When you work full speed forget all about form—just think of yourself as a gun shooting bullets at a target.

Remember: how you train is exactly how you will react under attack!

---

[1]Color video tapes are available of Sensei (Instructor) Sidney Filson teaching empty hand combinations. For information, send self-addressed, stamped envelope and write to her care of GRANT, 401 East 74th Street, Suite 4C, New York, New York 10021.

ATTACK FROM THE REAR

We are all susceptible to this form of attack, no matter how well-trained and aware we try to stay. The attacker may have monitored your movements for a long time and know your everyday routine. Or it may just be your bad luck to be in that place at that time. The reasons make no difference; you must deal with the situation.

The Actual Grab

The attacker will probably try to cover your mouth so your scream won't be heard. This is standard procedure and will actually help you defend yourself! In order to cover your mouth, the attacker must lift his elbow. *This exposes his vulnerable breathing system.* Therefore, *when attacked from behind you must always defend yourself on the side which covers your mouth.* The assailant's other hand will come around your body to contain any movement on your part.

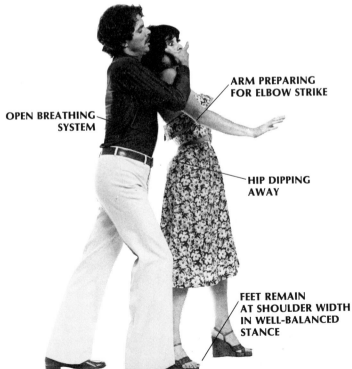

OPEN BREATHING SYSTEM

ARM PREPARING FOR ELBOW STRIKE

HIP DIPPING AWAY

FEET REMAIN AT SHOULDER WIDTH IN WELL-BALANCED STANCE

66

Do not wait to react until the grip on your mouth is firm! If you even sense a hand coming from behind, it is time to go into action!

Dip your hip away to further expose his breathing system, and prepare for an elbow strike. Hip and hand motion must occur simultaneously, balance must be maintained at all costs.

First Strike—Elbow into the Breathing System

Your hip has been dipped away to clear the path for your well-practiced elbow strike into the solar plexus (breathing system). The breathing system is one of the most delicate areas of the human body. It makes no difference how much your attacker weighs. His vulnerable areas are just as delicate as yours.

FULLY EXECUTED ELBOW STRIKE TO BREATHING SYSTEM

EYES ON ATTACKER

HAND READY FOR ACTION (TO BLOCK OR STRIKE)

KNEES FLEXED

BALANCE IS MAINTAINED

You must commit yourself fully to this elbow strike: tentative motion means nothing. Remember, your focus point is the back of his spine. How are you getting there? Through his breathing system!

If it is winter and your attacker wears heavy clothing, some of your hit power will be absorbed. Therefore, assume the worst. This first strike in the combination must be devastating! It is your only way to escape from his grip.

Always try to see where you are striking if possible (note that I have twisted my body as much as possible toward my assailant).

Your non-working hand is set in a protective position, ready for action. Should a change occur, this guarding hand would allow you to block a blow. **67**

WHIPLASH EFFECT

EYES ON
ASSAILANT

FULL SPEED
RISING PALM HEEL
UNDER CHIN

FOR FULL EXECUTION,
ELBOW MIGHT STRAIGHTEN
SLIGHTLY MORE,
BUT ALWAYS
KEEP SOME FLEX

OTHER HAND
READY FOR
NEXT STRIKE

BODY CLOSE
TO ATTACKER

FEET BALANCED
SHOULDER-WIDTH
APART

Second Strike—Palm Heel under the Chin

The elbow strike is immediately followed by a upward palm heel strike
under the chin, accompanied by a loud yell of spirit. This technique will cause
a whiplash shock which is immobilizing. If the strike connects with the side or
front of the attacker's face, that's fine too. As long as you give it all you've got,
your palm heel will be totally effective. Your other hand is now naturally
prepared for your next strike. Note that I have stayed close to the attacker
where defense is easier. *Never back up.* Your personal safety lies in being close
to every vulnerable area.

The scream must be given its full due as a technique. It will cause shock and
panic as you inflict pain in confusing patterns and may bring help!

68

Third Strike—Palm Heel to the Groin

Immediately deliver a strong, speedy, palm heel strike to the groin. Remember, your target point is the base of the spine. How do you get there? Through the pelvic structure! This palm heel is accompanied by another yell of spirit.

Now run! You have executed your combination. Do not stay around to see how it worked. Your attacker will now be in pain, shock, and confusion. Leave! Go to safety.

Your fighting combination has attacked middle, high, then low. You have struck with devastating speed. There is no way an assailant could anticipate the patterns you have used.

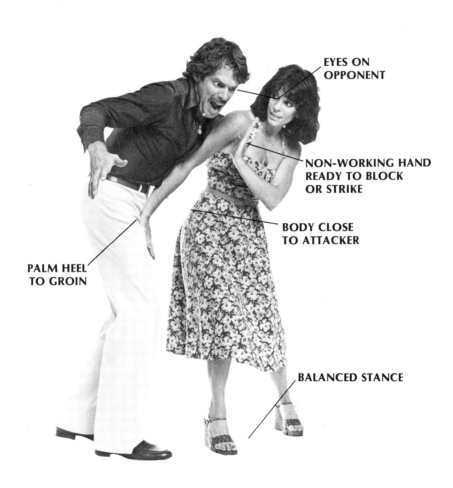

EYES ON OPPONENT

NON-WORKING HAND READY TO BLOCK OR STRIKE

BODY CLOSE TO ATTACKER

PALM HEEL TO GROIN

BALANCED STANCE

Working with a Partner

In practicing the back grab combination the attacking partner should actually grab you (in slow motion). This is the only way for you to develop the timing required. Making sure to dip your hip away to create the proper opening, execute all three strikes one after the other, smoothly and in very slow motion. Have your partner cover your mouth from the right and then from the left side. You must be able to defend yourself from both sides with equal coordination. Each of you should work fifty times at defending from a rear attack (twenty-five on each side). Then, standing side by side, both pretend an attacker is grabbing you. Shoot everything you've got, at full power and with a full yell of spirit, into the air behind you. Picture an assailant. Repeat twenty-five times on each side.

Please check your form carefully while practicing. Work this combination thousands of times. The oftener you repeat this pattern, the more reflexive it will become. Being scared or under pressure will only give you more speed and make you more devastating. You will not have to think if you are attacked from behind. Your training will work for you—self-defense will be automatic.

Working Alone

Imagine an attacker. Practice twenty-five times in slow motion on the left side; twenty-five times in slow motion on the right. Then at full speed, repeat twenty-five times on the right, twenty-five times on the left.

ATTACK FROM THE SIDE

The Actual Grab

"You're coming with me now!" or "You're going to enjoy this baby, so just keep quiet." are typical phrases an attacker uses when grabbing you from the side. He may try to pull you with him or push you backward. His grip might be a bit lower (wrist and elbow). Whatever the variations, you must defend against the side attack swiftly with a well-practiced combination.

FRONT ARM RAISED
TO BLOCK IF NECESSARY

EYES ON
OPPONENT

BACK HAND
PREPARED FOR
STRIKING

STANDING
LEG
REMAINS
FLEXED
AT KNEE

KICK TO LEG
CLOSEST TO YOU

RETAIN
BALANCE

First Strike—Kick to the Knee

With the leg nearest your attacker, deliver *from high chamber* a full-speed, downward-thrusting kick to just below his kneecap. Your front arm rises protectively—your back hand prepares for palm heel striking. *All of your motions occur simultaneously.* Use a loud yell of spirit!

Which kick you use depends on the position of your bodies at the moment of attack. If the attacker stands at a three-quarter angle to you, use your leg check. Either way, the contact is devastating to the attacker. You are striking a weak breaking-point at full speed! You have the added boost of a shoe. If you make contact an inch higher or an inch lower your technique will still be just as effective.

The pain of the quick kick plus the effect of raising your front arm will probably cause him to release his grip. As you...

71

EYES ON
OPPONENT

BOTH ARMS READY
TO STRIKE OR
DEFEND (BLOCK)

KEEP
KNEE
FLEXED

RETAIN
BALANCE

STOMP TO ARCH

Second Strike—Stomp Kick to Arch

. . . continue your kick on its downward path, scraping hard and fast against the sensitive shin bone, ending in a full power stomp on the metatarsal arch. This is another bone-breaking technique as the arch of the foot is very weak.

Third Strike—Palm Heel to the Face

Move in and throw a swift palm heel to center face. Contain his arms with your other hand.

The palm heel strike shoots right from the protective position. At this stage you no longer need to deliver from a chamber. Your earlier practice will have developed the power and focus of your blow. Your attacker may be falling from the kicks you delivered. If so, shoot the palm strike lower and still strike the center of his face. As long as you keep your eyes on your opponent you will be able to vary any technique to compensate for changes in body position.

Run to safety. Your attacker should now have a non-functioning suspension system and damage to his face mask. It is doubtful that he could pursue you, but take no chances—leave.

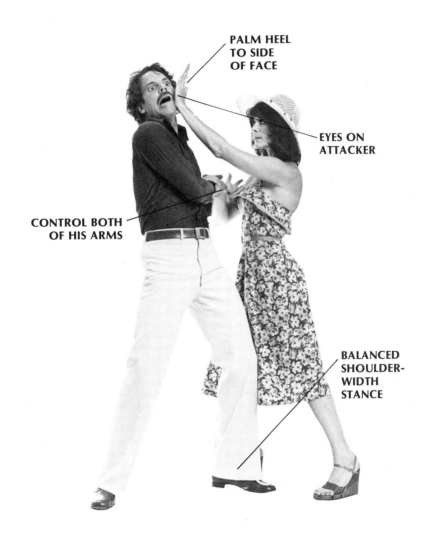

PALM HEEL
TO SIDE
OF FACE

EYES ON
ATTACKER

CONTROL BOTH
OF HIS ARMS

BALANCED
SHOULDER-
WIDTH
STANCE

Working with a Partner

In practicing the side grab combination the attacking partner should actually grab you in very slow motion, taking extreme care to *execute perfect form.* You should each defend from the right side twenty-five times and from the left side twenty-five times. You must always be prepared to defend from both sides. Next, both of you should work full speed in the air, pretending an attacker is grabbing you. Make sure you use your screams. Repeat twenty-five times on each side.

Work this side grab combination with the leg check kick and the heel kick. Get used to using both kicks in this combination. Ten thousand repetitions would not be too many.

Working Alone

Imagine an attacker. Repeat twenty-five times slow motion left side, twenty-five times slow motion right side. Then full speed, repeat twenty-five times on each side.

FRONT CHOKE ATTACK

The Actual Attack

Statistics show that most female murders are accomplished by strangulation from the front. Blackout occurs almost as soon as air is cut off at the windpipe.

Never allow anyone to put his hands on your throat! If you see an attack coming, your reaction must start *before* you feel any contact. If contact is the first awareness of a front choke, you have half a second to function successfully in defense of your life.

I have been choked to unconsciousness. The feeling is one of complete helplessness—like being down a long tunnel from what is happening. It happened to me as part of my training, not as an attack on my life. But what a shock, to realize how quickly one can lose consciousness.

So, if you see hands coming for your throat or if you feel hands around your throat, immediately...

First Strike—Finger Jab to the Eyes

Move in and thrust to the back of the skull through your attacker's eyes, screaming full-force as you strike.

JAB DIRECTLY
INTO EYES

EYES FOCUSED
ON TARGET

LOUD
SCREAM
WILL BOOST
YOUR POWER

OTHER HAND
COMES TO DEFENSIVE
POSITION

RETAIN
BALANCE

STEP FORWARD

Moving in is the most important part of this strike. Your attacker will probably be taller than you. The only way you will reach his eyes is by advancing. *If you stay put and fire a leading finger jab, the extension of his arms will prevent you from making contact* and all will be lost. Right leg and right finger jab work together. Left leg and left finger jag work together.

This attacker is attempting to kill you—strike with all your adrenaline. You must totally disable him!

75

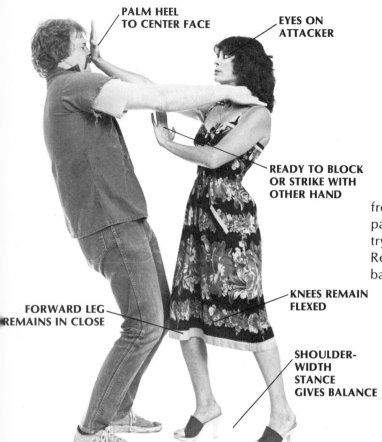

PALM HEEL TO CENTER FACE

EYES ON ATTACKER

READY TO BLOCK OR STRIKE WITH OTHER HAND

FORWARD LEG REMAINS IN CLOSE

KNEES REMAIN FLEXED

SHOULDER-WIDTH STANCE GIVES BALANCE

Second Strike—
Palm Heel to the Center Face

Without removing your fingers from the attacker's eyes, snap your palm heel down and forward. Again try to reach the back of his skull. Remain close to the attacker—do not back up!

GRAB AS STRONGLY AS POSSIBLE

EYES ON TARGET

SCREAM

RISING KNEE TO GROIN

BEND OTHER KNEE SLIGHTLY

Third Strike—
Rising Knee to the Groin

Grab him hard and hold on firmly as you bring up your knee with all you've got. Make sure you are deep between his legs. Make sure your standing leg is well bent. Balance is of supreme importance here; you must not waver—wearing high heels makes it even more important to flex your knee.

FIRM
HEAD GRIP

EYES FOCUSED

KNEE TO FACE

KNEE BENT
FOR BALANCE

Fourth Strike—Rising Knee to the Center Face

Grab the attacker's hair or the back of his head and bring his head down as your knee rises. Throw his body away from you and run!

I have given you four techniques in this combination since this type of attack is the most threatening to your life. If strike one is not enough, strike two will stop him; if that's not strong enough, strike three is devastating and so on.

This combination teaches you to use overkill. You are going to be so practiced, fast, and proficient at this series of techniques that an onlooker would not be able to see what strikes you use to defend yourself. Speed, timing, and focus all brought into play at once are more than any attacker can handle. Your strikes are hitting high then low into the body's most tender areas.

Working with a Partner

Defend yourself from a *full choke* on your neck *and from an approaching choke*. Use slow motion! Make sure you *move forward on your first strike.* This is a dangerous combination, so work very slowly. Build a good flow from one technique to the other. Work on both sides of your body. Each partner must defend thirty-five times with right finger jab start and thirty-five times with left finger jab start. Alternate defending from full choke and approaching choke. Then, both partners must work full speed in the air. Race each other to completion: repeat thirty-five times on each side.

Working Alone

Imagine an attacker. Practice thirty-five times in slow motion on the left side; repeat thirty-five times in slow motion on the right. At full speed, repeat thirty-five times on each side.

I have given you more repetitions of this combination than of any other. You must be as programmed as a computer. This frontal attack allows you less time to defend yourself than any other. Onlookers are always amazed by the speed with which my students execute this series of strikes. They would be just as amazed to find out how many hours the students had drilled to achieve the confident expertise they display. Their speed is no accident but the result of thousands of careful repetitions. I expect you to be swift and accurate.

Here are some rules for actual use of combinations in self-defense:

- Always use an entire combination when defending yourself. One technique is never good enough, even if you think it was a knockout. Complete your entire series. I don't care if you end up firing into the air while your opponent is unconscious at your feet. You are going to be so fast that the few seconds it takes to throw all the strikes in the combination will make no difference. Nothing must be left to chance where your life is concerned.
- Once you are in action, every move must be a strike.
- Commit yourself 100 percent. Once you've made a decision do not hesitate; I want you to become an advancing locomotive and go for broke!
- Let the adrenaline happen! You will not freeze up from it—your reflexes will take over and you will throw all your adrenaline at your attacker with screams and strikes.
- Be ready for change. Your attacker may be closer than you had anticipated. Instead of a palm heel strike, you would use an elbow or a monkey knee. Never be locked into any pattern; flexibility must be one of your self-defense talents.
- Your eyes must always see all of your attacker at once. You may be striking into his face and seeing that, but you must also be using peripheral vision to see his feet. You can do this easily; just make sure you do it in practice.

Weapons SIX

I've listened to many police accounts of crimes against women and have studied crime statistics. I also have an extensive collection of first-hand accounts by women who've been attacked and robbed; one-quarter of the women who come to me for self-defense training have been violently attacked. By accumulating this knowledge, I have formed opinions that determine which techniques I teach women for self-defense. These tales of terror have made me sure of one fact; a woman needs a weapon!

Attackers have weapons. They wield knives with expertise. They have guns. They threaten with hammers and screwdrivers, tire irons and icepicks. Some criminals have deadly imaginations. One woman who was robbed, raped, and beaten had been intimidated by her attacker who told her the can marked "lye" would finish off her good looks for life if she resisted.

THE KEY CHAIN

I have developed a weapon especially for you. It has several advantages. Deadly and accurate, it does not look like a weapon and may be carried openly. It is inexpensive to make. Learning to use it is easy, and you can utilize it to defend yourself against more than one attacker. There is no law against possessing this form of protection, and its maintenance is simple. This weapon has a valid everyday function so you have a practical reason for carrying it. I refer to a key chain—a bit heavier than most, certainly with more keys than most—but still a key chain. My weapon has saved my life.[1] I am never without it. You should never be without yours.

MAKING YOUR WEAPON

Go to a pet shop and purchase a twelve-inch choke collar. It should have a sturdy chain and a metal ring at each end.

[1]Color video tapes of Sensei Filson teaching the use of her key chain weapon are available. For information write to her care of GRANT, 401 East 74th Street, Suite 4C, New York, New York 10021, and send a self-addressed, stamped envelope.

Next go to a hardware store; *purchase the strongest spiral metal key ring they* have. It should be about one and one-half inches in diameter. *Make sure it is a double circle ring*, the kind that requires you to slip the key between pressed-together metal rings, then turn until the key becomes free in the center of the circle. This is the only type of ring you should use. I have found no substitute. While you are at the hardware store, ask for old keys. They are usually available for nothing. Take all the keys they will give you.

Put the key ring on one of the metal loops at the end of the dog collar. Mark your own keys with a bit of red nail polish and place them on the ring. Now hang all the extra keys on that ring. The heavier the weight of the key chain, the better it will serve you as a weapon. I have two rings full of keys on my chain. I have also added a small, oblong piece of lead. It looks like a name plate but is actually there as a weight to boost striking power. Some of my students hang fishing weights along with keys for extra heft.

Once your chain is hooked up, *pull on it. Try to pull it apart. Subject it to stress. Make sure it is strong and will hold together.* You may have to use this weapon to save your life. Test it carefully.

In the years I have been openly carrying this weapon, no one has ever realized that it's a fighting instrument. When I get on an elevator, it is always in my hand.[2] Men often comment on it: "You've got the keys to the kingdom there," "Do you have doors for all those keys?"; or, "Are you a chamber maid?" If I feel the need to explain my chain I smile and say, "It's easy to find in my bag" (which it is). If a woman comments, I usually tell her it's a weapon. This arouses her interest and often leads to another self-defense student.

Even a mugger lying in wait for you would not be aware that the key chain is a deadly weapon. The criminal assumes the keys are in your hand in preparation for opening your door. Many people reach for their keys long before they are at their door. Some people swing keys around as a habit. No one will know you are armed. That's the beauty of your weapon.

In learning to use your weapon never put your fingers through the empty ring at the end of the chain. That should dangle freely as you *grip the chain with a fist.* Your grip should be very firm. No one should be able to jerk it away from you. Your thumb will exercise control.

[2]My statistical research shows that an elevator is the most dangerous place for women.

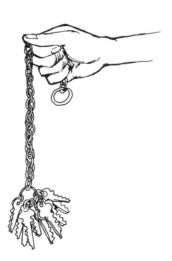

The first movement you will learn with your weapon will be "figure eights." The figure-eight pattern you will follow will be lying on its side. The center of that figure eight (where an "X" is formed) will be directly in front of you. Like your empty hand strikes or your kicks, your weapon must be centered. That center is your striking point, i.e., the place where your keys will actually contact the target. Within a figure-eight pattern there are two strikes: one at the center of the forward swing, one at the center of the backward swing.

In order to avoid hitting yourself, you must *keep your arm extended in front of you during the entire figure-eight pattern. Your elbow must always remain in front of your center line as your arm swings the weapon.*

Your whole arm works the weapon. Do not use only your wrist. Your arm turns over to work the figure eights. Your palm faces down on the downward swing. Your palm faces up on the return swing. Even though all this turning is going on, remember to *keep your elbow in front of your own center.*

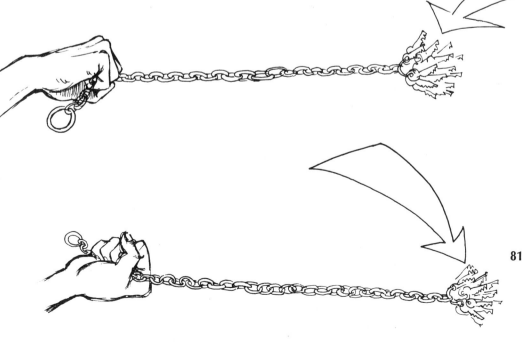

81

Your objective—in addition to striking your opponent—is to form a whirling, fan-like protection in front of you.

Anything trying to get through that fast-moving barrier would either be hit or deflected. Both results are to your advantage. So, *when you are working your figure eight, make sure you are putting up an effective blocking device* with your weapon.

1. Work on your figure-eight pattern for *five minutes with each hand.* Yes, you must be able to use this weapon effectively with both hands. What if you have an injury to the hand you ordinarily use? Is that to stop you from functioning and protecting yourself?

2. *Work your chain for an extra minute with whichever hand is the weaker.*

3. *Work on the same figure eight to your side.* Now your rib cage becomes your center line. All the same rules apply. Keep your arm out. Look where you strike. *Change to your other side and hand. Spend five minutes on stronger side, six minutes on weaker side.* Imagine an attacker; strike to his head.

Be careful to keep your arm extended. Know where you're striking. See!

As soon as you feel familiar with your weapon, start walking and even running while practicing. I want you to be able to defend yourself from all sides while moving swiftly.

Striking Across

All that is required for learning this strike is *not to bend your elbow.* If you do, you will be hit in the head for sure, so do not bend your elbow on the strike across.

1. *Stand as you would on the street with your weapon in one hand. Now look to the side as though someone were approaching you. Lift your hand and strike back and forth in a straight line at your imaginary opponent's head. Do not bend your elbow. Still keeping your arm straight, lower it back to your side.*

2. *Work this strike five minutes on stronger side, six minutes on weaker side.*

Working with a partner You must work even more slowly on straight strike across than you did with your empty-hand defenses. This is dangerous work. *Have your partner approach you from the side and grab your shoulder. Slowly, slowly execute the strike across as your partner pulls her head out of the way.* You both know what is coming, so anticipate it when you are playing the attacker. Pull your head well back, so you won't get hit. Now have your partner approach you from the other side. *Practice ten times on each side.*

Striking to the Rear
You must know how to fight behind you with your key chain. Rear attacks are common and may be dealt with easily if you know how.

1. *Stand with your weapon at your side.*

2. *With right hand, swing keys across your back and catch them with your left hand* (behind your back).

3. *Now swing keys across your body to your front left side. Catch them with left hand. Go slowly at first,* so you don't bang up your back. It is important that you learn to sense the whereabouts of your weapon at all times. This exercise will teach it to you. Imagine someone holding you from behind. This exercise will teach you general dexterity with your weapon.

Practice five minutes on stronger side. Six minutes on weaker side.

Don't work with a partner on this strike. It is too dangerous. This is what would happen if an attacker met with your weapon on a sneaky approach.

Striking to the Groin

All this strike requires is a simple upswing. *Practice five minutes on each side.*

Striking to the Knees

If you are knocked to the ground, a straight swing to the knees would disable your attacker.

Stabbing

Practice screaming as you strike.

1. *Grip your keys in right hand. Hold chain in left. Step forward and stab on your own center line, screaming as you strike.*

Practice twenty times, alternating sides. Use a strong yell of spirit with each strike.

Working with a partner
1. *Face each other in shoulder-width stances.*
2. *Attacking partner raises her hands as though to choke you.*

Practicing key chain throat strike.

3. *You grab keys in the stabbing manner and, in very slow motion make one straight line to center of attacker's face. Stop one inch from her face.*

When practicing with a partner, don't allow the choke to be placed on your throat. You wouldn't allow that in reality; don't do it in practice. Remember the front choke is the most dangerous of all holds—most female deaths by violence are caused by frontal strangulation. (See front choke combinations in chapter five.)

Repeat twenty times in slow motion, alternating hands.

Repeat twenty times, aiming for the throat and alternating hands.

4. *Get on the ground as though you had been knocked down. Have your partner approach you slowly. Grip your keys in the stabbing manner and strike, in slow motion, for the groin.* Stop one inch from your target!

Repeat twenty times in slow motion, alternating hands.

5. Repeat ground work, *this time for the knees.* You may strike them from the front or side.

The most important thing about learning to use your key chain is your total understanding of your own weapon. Play with it. Aim it. Swing it. Stab with it. Get to know your weapon. Try hanging two rings full of keys on it. See if you don't get a different, perhaps better, mobility. It's your weapon—personalize it. You may come up with a whole new way of using it or a variation that will improve on these methods. (If so, do write to me, so I can pass along good ideas to my students.)

Once you are totally familiar with your own weapon, I would suggest getting a *metal police whistle* and hanging it on the free ring at the end of your chain. These whistles produce a terrific blast, terrifying to someone in the midst of a criminal act.

The whistle may also be used in a stabbing manner (the same as the front choke defense with bunched up keys). Having a whistle means that you have a loud yell of spirit at the end of your weapon.

I don't want you to depend on the whistle, though. Just think of the blasting sound as an added attraction. You still must concentrate on stunning your attacker and stopping his advance. You may not have time to use the whistle in an emergency, but it is definitely a good thing to have on your key chain (and wonderful for attracting cabs in big cities).

THE PLASTIC SPRAY BOTTLE

A plastic bottle with a pump spray attached (such as a window or household cleaner container) may be *filled with ammonia* and carried or kept by your bedside as an effective deterrent to a mugger or house-breaker. The container should be refilled with ammonia frequently to make sure the contents are full-strength.

If you are forced to use this blinding liquid in your own defense, *don't hesitate!* Once you make a decision, exercise full commitment immediately! A moment of hesitation could mean the difference between life and death.

The spray should be directed at the attacker's eyes, and you must *keep* spraying until your assailant has grabbed his eyes, and you are sure you can get away.

I am not going to teach you to disarm an attacker in this book. That requires an expert martial art teacher working *with* the student. I do not believe you can learn the necessary techniques from a book, no matter how astute you are.

But with proper training you are capable of disarming—any woman is.

I teach my students the mechanics of disarming and tell them at what point they are actually capable of applying them to a real life situation.

If you are interested in learning disarming techniques, train only with an expert; this is nothing to fool around with—these are life and death situations.

SEVEN

How to Act in Specific Situations

There are dangerous emotional and physical situations you, as a woman, are likely to find yourself in at one time or another. Just knowing what is really dangerous may make it possible for you to avoid them. But if you do find yourself in the middle of a nightmare, it is imperative to know how to pull yourself together, face the situation head on, and get through it alive and sane. Let's look at some of the tricky turns life's path can take and how to make it through unscathed.

WHEN YOU HAVE TO SAY "NO"

A main theme of assertiveness training programs for women is learning the simple word, "NO." Grown women turn red in the face trying to overcome the guilt they feel saying "no" and when I ask them why, "I feel as though I'm insulting someone," or, "It just doesn't seem nice," are typical answers. Perhaps the most common answer is, "I feel guilty because I don't have a good enough reason for saying no. My only excuse is that I don't want to."

That is a *good* reason, the perfect reason, and one everyone is fully entitled to!

Between you and me, saying "no" is a wonderful feeling. It gives me a sensation of freedom and a release from pressure. But to release that pressure fully, it must not be accompanied by excuses! A "no, thank you" is sufficient. (It's always best to be polite.) Let's look at a situation which might require you to take a stand.

You've been out to dinner with a new friend. You've had a lovely evening and it's time to go home. He asks you to stop by his apartment for a nightcap. You really don't want to. But, as is your custom, you lie and make excuses: "I'd love to, but I have to get up early in the morning." His rejoinder might be: "We won't stay long." Then you make another excuse: "Well, my morning meeting is important, and I have to do some preparatory research before I go." He comes back with: "C'mon, you're smart enough to handle all that; I really want

88

you to see my apartment—I promise we'll just stay a few minutes." This goes on and on until you give in rather than take a firm stand and say "no."

You made the whole procedure complicated and ended up doing something you didn't want to. That is wrong. Let's go back and start from the beginning, and I'll write the script.

Friend: Let's stop by my apartment for a nightcap.

You: No, thank you. (Accompanied by a pleasant attitude.)

Friend: But, I want to show you my digs.

You: No, thanks, I'd like to go home now. (Again, the pleasant attitude.)

Now "friend" is either going to be a gentleman and say cheerfully, OK, we'll make it another time; I'll take you home now, or he's going to press. Pressing is a game; it could go like this:

Friend: Why? Don't you like me? Do you think I would try to do something wrong?

You: I just don't want to.

If "friend" gets an attitude and waxes huffy, he's *not* a friend. He should have told you that the dinner invitation included a stop by his home afterward. If he's a nice person, he will accept your true feelings and respect you for stating them openly and forthrightly. Remember, making unnecessary excuses shows weakness and indecision. Anyone who senses that will continue to push you.

You are not obligated to explain why you said "no." Neither are you obligated to do anything you do not want to! Your only duty is to yourself. If you find yourself in a situation where you are uncomfortable, be honest with yourself and leave. That's the whole key—honesty.

I find it interesting to say "no" nicely and then watch the reaction of the questioner. Usually they wait for further words from me. They can't believe that's the end of the answer. Sometimes they say "What?" I repeat my "no."

So many women let themselves be pushed into corners and made to feel uncomfortable. They experience moments they truly dislike because of a foolish reluctance to say "no."

Don't let this happen to you. Say "no" and enjoy taking the weight off your shoulders. The lifting of the mental load will transfer into a physical spring in your step. I promise you.

So, if you've been feeling pressured because of this particular problem, break the pattern. What can happen? The person will be insulted and storm away? So what? That's not someone you would want to know better, in business or pleasure—you're better off without knowing him. Do you feel you might lose a chance for a business deal? I like the Zen philosophy that tells us "you will lose nothing in this life you are meant to have."

I was once being considered for a role in a film that I wanted very much. The interviewer asked me to discuss the possibilities of playing the role over cocktails that evening. I had previously made a personal rule never to socialize with business associates. I looked him square in the eye, smiled nicely, and told him: "No, thank you, I'm available to discuss business only during office hours." And, I figured, there goes that part.

I was surprised when my agent called and told me I had the role. She said the man had commented on his admiration for me because I had not made excuses for my feelings, a rare thing in his experience. So, I was meant to have that part, and I was able to work as a professional with no pressure.

Let's take the worst that a firm "no" could get you. A punch. That's right, what if someone tried by physical power to force you to do what he wanted? Then it's time to back up word power with "hit power." That's all. Use your blocking system.

As long as you can back up a "no," if need be, you don't ever have to be afraid to come up with a firm negative.

THE MEN ON THE STREETS

When a woman walks by a bunch of construction workers, or a group of friends hanging out on a street corner, she is usually subjected to cat-calls, whistles, and semi-lascivious remarks.

There is no physical harm in this form of male group play. You may be personally insulted, but there is no immediate danger to your person. The men are busy impressing each other.

How you feel about it usually depends on your mood. If it's been a rough day at the office, you may be offended and get mad. On the other hand, if you're in a good mood, you may be complimented by the attention.

Regardless of how you feel, on the streets it is wise to keep your feelings to yourself. Just continue about your business.

THE MAN WHO CURSES AT YOU ON THE STREET

I often see this in big cities. It has happened to me. A man will come up to a woman on the street for no apparent reason and shout obscenities right into her face: "You motherfucking cunt;" "No good bitch." Or, perhaps it is ethnic cursing: "You white whore;" "Nigger bitch."

You will, of course, be taken aback if this happens to you. It is shocking. Here is a stranger, shouting at you. The language in itself, if you're not used to cursing, is hard to handle.

Walk away and show no emotion. Have your hand on your key chain; be prepared to whirl and block and strike should he come after you.

Let's break this down so you understand the psychology behind your actions.

The man is goading you, for whatever reason—he had a fight with his wife, he hates his mother, he is mentally unstable. He may want to get your attention, to initiate an emotional experience such as a fight or a rape—something violent to relieve the tremendous tensions he's built up. So, the potential attacker sees a woman (or a child or an older person) obviously weaker than he, as prey. The basic premise: the weak feed on the weaker, and if they look weak, they probably are. Here is exactly how you should react:

1. *Don't respond to goading.* Any response gives fuel to the antagonist! Most important for your safety is that you *not give a fear response.* Remember, *non-response is not a fear reaction.* Anything else would be over-reacting and could further excite him or turn him off; you can't tell. For example, if the woman yelled at him, "Fuck you!" in a Master Sergeant's voice, it could cause a reaction either way.

2. *Continue on your non-collision course with your awareness button turned to the "on" position.* (His behavior will have triggered your adrenaline anyway.)

3. *Keep going until the person is obviously coming to striking distance on a set course for you.* (Hear him, see him from the corner of your eye.)

4. *Apply a martial art solution, and make it a good one.* This guy is really going to try to hurt you. Strike swiftly at every opening you see—he deserves whatever he gets.

5. *Leave.*

PUBLIC TRANSPORTATION AND THE EMBARRASSMENT FACTOR

Public vehicles—and especially terminals and waiting areas—are a favorite haunt of molesters. These creatures who get a kick out of grabbing and pinching women in public places know exactly what they are doing. The perverse pleasure they receive from the physical act is boosted by the confused and quiet reaction of their victims. It is a fact that many women do not defend themselves because they are embarrassed by the attention their actions might draw. *Don't ever be embarrassed. It is foolish. No one should be allowed to touch your body against your will.*

What you should do if someone touches you in public is turn the tables; embarrass *him*. For example, imagine you are sitting on a subway or bus and a man puts his hand on your leg. Instead of remaining silent out of embarrassment, you should say in a *loud* voice, "Get your hand off my leg." He will be embarrassed and try to pretend you're not addressing him. Or he might make a face-saving remark, such as, "You must be crazy lady." That's OK. Let him play his game. Just fix a steely eye on him. Let him know you're not going to stand for any nonsense.

If he is unwise enough to persist and touch you again, it is time to take action. *Push pins are great for this particular breed of molester* but *only if he is acting on the "sneak,"* i.e. if he is touching you while faking an innocent look for the benefit of the other passengers.

Quickly thrust a push pin into the back of his hand—the hand that's on your leg—and move to another seat. *Keep your awareness of him, even though you have moved away.*

I have done that under exactly those circumstances. The man was paralyzed with disbelief. All he could do was stare at the push pin stuck in the back of his hand. From the look on his face I surmised he was experiencing pain, confusion, and fear. His fear may have been of pulling the pin out and not knowing whether or not it had a barb. Perhaps he thought there was poison on the pin. Who knows? At any rate, he had no time to think about me, just his hand and his own embarrassment. He hid the whole incident from the other passengers. I was fully prepared to deal with him if he had got up and come after me. As a matter of fact, I had positioned myself for just that eventuality, **91** *with my trusty key chain in my hand*, camouflaged by my pocket.

If the man persists boldly—if he puts his hand on you again after your public verbal blast and returns your direct gaze—you have a problem. This man is challenging you directly and infringing on your sacred, personal privacy. Calling for help will do you no good, unless there is a policeman within sight. If you choose to stop him at this time, there are plenty of good techniques to apply to the situation. Here are a few combinations you might use, keeping in mind that you are sitting next to each other, side by side:

1. Grab his pinky finger *very firmly* and *quickly* bend it *all the way back* to the back of his hand. (The finger will easily break.)

2. Drive a good, sharp elbow strike into his ribs (breathing system).

3. Deliver a palm heel to the side-center of his face.
   or:
1. With your bunched-up key chain use a full-force downward stab to the back of his hand.
2. Quickly strike to the side of his face or throat with the bunched-up key chain.
3. Strike into the ribs with the bunched-up key chain.
   or:
1. Direct your palm heel to the side-center of his face.
2. Kick his knee (from side or front).
3. Stomp hard on the metatarsal arch of his foot.

These are only a few of the combinations you could put together with the knowledge you have accumulated. There are innumerable ways of stringing together the techniques you now have in your repertoire. I have given you only a few examples.

The important thing in a situation like this is to *know what techniques you are going to use.* This is not a sudden attack; you were forewarned by his first touch. Now you are the target for a second bold touch. Choose a combination in your mind, and go ahead with it. Quickly! Now is the time for speed, proper placement of strikes, and full commitment on your part. Reach for that chamber when you use your elbows; you know how.

If you use your form properly, your combinations *will* work. The strikes you are using and, particularly the striking patterns, are foreign to your molester. Most women, if they tried to hit, would slap at him or take one punch. You are attacking in a martial art manner, fully aware of what you are doing. This is your advantage and the reason why you have bothered to learn these things.

Your only other alternative is to sit there and let him do whatever he wants. Or you might appeal to other passengers to help you. How you handle the situation is up to you, but it is good to have choices.

93

You can practice sitting combinations with a partner. Just sit side by side on a bench, couch, or two chairs and, in slow motion, practice the different strike combinations both with your key chain and your empty hand. See what you can come up with on your own. The variations are unlimited.

I do not feel that this type of situation calls for eye-jabbing techniques. Nor should you try to use empty-handed groin strikes. When someone is sitting at your side it is difficult to attack the pelvic area with the techniques now at your command. Only your bunched-up key chain would be a valid technique; but it would require a very fast, hard thrust through the pelvic structure to the end of the backbone.

You are safer with your combinations if you see a clear path to your striking points and follow it.

DRUG USERS AND HOW TO COPE WITH THEM

Dealing with a Drunk

This is specialized territory with its own set of rules. Even if you know the inebriated person well, you don't know him when he's drunk. Alcohol has the ability to turn pussycats into tigers.

First, *recognize the problem*—he is *drunk*. Don't delude yourself. Acknowledge the facts so that you can deal with them. Realize that the drunk does not know he is drunk. He is in another state, seeing the world and you from a distorted viewpoint.

Try to avoid interpersonal contact or encouragement. If this is impossible, your next step is guile. Kidding along can often dispense with the whole situation. A drunk has wide mood swings, and a joke can bring him from mad to glad in a second.

If guile doesn't work, *display coldness accompanied by a firm "no" in a conversational tone of voice.* If this doesn't get through the "drunk umbrella," if you're in a situation where you can't leave, if he's holding you or trying to do you harm, *you will have to deal with him by physical force.*

Know that he is anesthetized by alcohol and will not feel pain on the same level as a person who is not under the influence. You will have to deal differently with a drunk.

"Shove shock is the greatest technique for dealing with drunks, particularly because they end up hurting themselves and you can't really get indicted or prosecuted too badly for that," says Grand Master Peter Urban.

Shove shock is taught in chapter three. *Use it to knock a drunk off his feet,* but be prepared to deal with blind violent rage if he is able to get up. That means *you must knock him out.* (If he is violent in the first place, skip shove shock and concentrate on a knockout.)

To knock out a drunk *strike the solar plexus or under it. Second choice would be the windpipe.* In other words, *concentrate on the breathing system.* Even if someone is beyond feeling pain, he cannot function without air! (If you have time to check his breathing pattern, try to hit his diaphragm when he is inhaling.) Use a palm heel strike, an elbow, or a knee, and *go for the backbone.*

94

Shove shock as the initial technique has these advantages: no one can be anesthetized against it, and it takes advantage of the *off-balance state of the drunk*. The sound of breaking furniture attracts attention, and if you are in a public place it means it's no longer a two-person affair.

Remember, alcohol is an aggressive encourager, and *the drunk is likely to fight.*

The "Up" User

An attacker under the influence of any of a great assortment of "ups" is a crazed adversary. Cocaine produces paranoia, and a user who is normally rational and friendly will suddenly change and assume that his closest friend has just called the police on him or is trying to murder him. This potent drug also makes users see things—shadows, ghosts, all sorts of illusions. The combination of liquor and cocaine produces the most violent feelings.

"Speed" comes in many assortments. Amphetamines (diet pills) turn users into babbling idiots. They undergo personality changes and, in advanced states, they will have spittle in the corners of their mouths. "Speed," like cocaine, produces paranoid delusions which make for violence.

An attacker under the influence of this group of drugs assaults for no particular reason. It doesn't have to be money or sex, just pure violence. Since this can occur even with a new user, there is a chance that this type of attacker is strong and fast as well as parnoid.

Pleading and showing weakness will not help since the user may be picturing you as the devil: someone he has to kill.

Understand that during this paranoia and "speeding," the user's heart is pumping very fast, his pulse rate is very high. *Go for the breathing-system knockout.* Do not try to inflict pain on this attacker, he won't feel it. If he is very high the drugs will even prevent him from feeling the pain of a broken bone.

Psychedelic Drug Users

LSD, mescaline, DMT, hog, etc. may all have "speed" mixed in with the hallucinogen; therefore *apply the same martial art solution used to deal with the "up" user*—strike the breathing-system.

The "Down" User

An attacker high from heroin, barbiturates (sleeping pills), or potent tranquilizers is on a "down." He is apt to be sleepy, off-balance, and seeing the world and you through a haze. He's got what he wants and should not be particularly violent. If he's holding you up, or trying to rape you, or just hanging himself all over you in an annoying manner, he should be dealt with the same as the drunk. He is also anesthetized. *He is a candidate for shove shock* and a *breathing-system knockout.*

I have seen these narcotics users in fights. They react very slowly and, if they do try to hit someone, it is usually with a slow-motion, overhead strike or a slow-motion, round-house strike (a punch that comes around from the side to hit you as opposed to a straight down the middle strike). These are blows easily avoided and countered.

95

But if the "down" user has not had his fix, he is an entirely different animal. He is nervous and desperate and will kill to obtain money in order to get drugs. He is very aware in a panicky way. This attacker should be cajoled and placated until the opportunity arises to strike. And you *must* strike; I have counseled many women horribly mutilated by addicts who got money and still did their dirty deed for no other reason than to hurt.

Personally, I would assume this type of attacker meant to kill me and act accordingly, using my strongest defenses. Finger jabbing to the eyes, striking to the windpipe and solar plexus, then kicking the knees is an example of a strike combination I would try to use.

Do remember, the "down" user is almost always in a weakened physical state. He is quite different from the drunk who can be really strong. Although the "down" user's verbal attack may be strong, his physical capabilities are limited. These drugs take a heavy toll on the heart, respiratory system, and all internal organs. Running away is usually easy as the narcotics user is not known for stamina. Cigarette smoking is part of the syndrome so his breathing system is probably already damaged.

THE NICE GUY YOU JUST MET

Here is one woman's terrifying story:

Jill was an adorable nineteen years old. She had a turned-up nose, big brown innocent eyes, a size three figure, and a continuous smile on her face. She was a very happy person with an infectious laugh. Jill was a delight to have around—one of my favorite students. She came to study and visit with me one summer. I got to know her well. There was a lot of work involved in her training. She had been overly pampered by her loving parents, continually waited on, and had not developed athletically. She was weak and tiny and I was working on developing her stamina. She was delicate and bruised easily. I knew that it would be a while before she would be able to defend herself. But Jill loved the training and had a good attitude.

One day, she called and told me she had met a terrific guy. He was a great big, good-looking, funny man. She had been out with him twice and was looking forward to a date that night. She thought he might be "the one." I was happy for her and told her to keep me informed and to be sure to invite me to the wedding.

Four days later, I received a phone call. Jill was being held by the police. She was on Riker's Island in New York. Her new friend had taken her to a murder! Jill was charged with conspiracy, kidnapping, and accessory to murder. She had been in jail since that night I had spoken to her. She had never stopped crying, and would not eat. It was a steaming August (the year of the black-out in New York). The temperature was steadily in the nineties, and the overcrowded jail must have been hell for that hysterical girl.

I knew there was no way Jill could willingly have been involved in a murder. I was her martial arts instructor. She couldn't even bring herself to throw a hard punch for fear she would harm one of her *dojo* sisters. I could not stop thinking of little Jill in that jail.

I got in touch with her parents (her dad was a doctor), and the family came immediately to New York. By the time they arrived, their daughter had been taken somewhere for interrogation. No one seemed to know where! After a full week of lawyers' and judges' intervening, Jill was found in a small town in New Jersey (where the alleged murder had occurred).

She had been taken to New Jersey illegally and had been interrogated steadily all that time. She still had not eaten, and it was a doctor's opinion that she would die if she were not put into a hospital. She had of course signed all sorts of statements agreeing to cooperate with district attorneys. While on Riker's Island she had been sexually assaulted several times by lesbians and had been badly beaten.

Jill was eventually vindicated. She had been an unwilling witness to a horror-filled nightmare. It was six months of hell for her and when it was over, her parents took her to Europe to finish college.

Schizophrenia is a mental disorder characterized by a separation of thought and emotions, by delusions and bizarre behavior. Violent, schizoid men can be most charming early in a relationship. A woman may be lulled into trusting her new friend completely and be caught totally unaware when the bomb explodes!

Check out new acquaintances. Most people with violent tendencies repeat their assault patterns, and lots of people know about the incidents. Talk to a new male friend; see if you don't have common friends. It's a small world. You can be clever and find out *something* about his character and background. This is not being nosy, but self-protective.

If a schizophrenic does go into a violent rage directed at you, (the slightest thing can trigger it) you must *immediately knock him out with a breathing-system combination.*

The stranger you're out with might not be a violent schizophrenic, but why subject yourself even to an unpleasant situation? Avoid any dilemma and *find out who the nice guy you just met is.*

BREAKING UP IS HARD TO DO

Ending a relationship often means making an enemy. A rejected lover can be a potential danger to a woman trying to say good-bye. Emotions run high when couples split, and the male outlet is often physical violence—directed at the female.

Police statistics show that most murders of females occur at the hands of someone they know well.

So if you've been in emotional conflict over a break-up, be careful. *A threat of physical violence should be taken seriously. Never get together for a "talk" at the suggestion of a man who has threatened you. Carry your key chain all the time*; it is easy for someone who knows your daily routines to accost you outside your home. See chapter six for a weapon you can make at home and *keep it by your bed at night. Remember, if you've lived with the person who is threatening you, he can probably get in your house!*

THE BATTERED WIFE

If you are being assaulted regularly by someone you know well, you have a terrific problem because you are battered physically *and psychologically.*

You need more than my book.

If you care to stay with this person who has been beating you and want to get the relationship back on an even keel, you have a tough job ahead of you.

I would suggest going to a martial art school where they have contact sparring in their classes. After all, you've been in full-contact receivership for a long time. You'll handle it better than a woman who hasn't been beaten.

Study secretly. Lie if you have to. Say you're going to a quilting class or cooking class—anything but the truth at this time.

Show yourself as a serious student in the martial arts school; then *inform your instructor of your problem.* He or she will be able to apply special tactics to your training. You will also have a psychological boost because there will be someone with whom you can discuss your dilemma. You will grow strong in this way, both mentally and physically.

You cannot fight this problem by yourself. If you continue to take these beatings, you risk becoming crippled, or you may kill your assailant out of fear. Either way is horrible for you.

Before embarking on a martial art solution to the problem, make sure you want it solved. I once had an hysterical student who called me every time her husband beat her. She had made the initial mistake of informing him that she was taking self-defense training. This put him on his guard, and he beat her more, taunting her with: "Where's your karate now?" I saw her often, and she usually sported a black eye and bruises on her body. We discussed the problem and each time it happened my student swore she was leaving him. I came to realize that there was a pattern to the whole affair. They would have a knock-down, drag-out fight; he would mark her up; then she would use the bruises to make him feel guilty. He would buy her a present, take her to dinner; then they would make mad, passionate love, and everything would be coming up roses—until the next fight. When I brought the facts to light in a discussion with this battered wife, she was appalled at being called a masochist. But that's what she was. She liked the argument; she liked being hit; she loved making up.

It is much easier to defend yourself against a stranger than someone you know.

The ideal solution would be to train like crazy, get strong and confident, and wait for the next attack. Then when he goes to strike, you would block his blow (you would know the pattern from past experience) and knock him out! When he woke up, tell him you will break his bones or kill him the next time. He would then begin to respect you again and you would be able to have a rational relationship. I seriously doubt you could bring yourself to this point.

Here is a more likely result: you will gain strength from your martial art training and no longer want to be with someone who beats you. In any case the only logical solution to this problem is to train the martial art way, secretly, and then reevaluate the situation from a physically and mentally stronger position.

COMBAT ZONES

Some areas are havens for muggers and rapists—and nightmares for women. It is important to know where the danger zones are and exactly how to act in them for your own protection. Like a well-trained soldier, you must proceed with extreme caution, your weapon at the ready—prepared for anything!

Elevators

There is no more dangerous place for a woman than an elevator. It is a moving trap, and just because you get into an empty elevator does not mean you are safe. That elevator can stop at any floor and admit your attacker. Just because there are a few people on the elevator with you does not mean you are safe. Those people can get off and leave you alone with a potential attacker. Just because you are not attacked in an elevator does not mean you are safe. Your attacker can spot you there and follow you off. Just because you have another woman with you does not mean you are safe. Two women post no more threat to an attacker than one.

Elevator muggers and rapists are clever and practiced. There is certainly no pattern or type of person typical of elevator assaults.

Melinda entered an elevator in her building. There were other passengers, among them a very good-looking, well-dressed young man carrying a bouquet of flowers. Melinda remembers thinking that some lucky lady lived in her building and wished it were she.

The time came when she and the handsome man were left alone in the elevator. He pulled a gun from within his bouquet of flowers and ordered her to get on her knees with her back to him. He took all her money and her jewelry; then he pushed the button for the nineteenth floor of her building. When the door opened on that floor he pushed her off.

Up until that point Melinda had not been scared. He was not nasty and had not hurt her. She figured he would take her money and leave. But now she was on the top floor of her building, and he was taking her toward the door that led to the roof. She panicked and screamed. Luckily for her, a resident of that floor opened his door. The gunman fled down the stairs.

Here are some *elevator rules* for you to follow:

- Whenever possible don't take elevators. Use the stairs. They are less dangerous statistically, and avenues of escape are available should you be attacked. Climbing stairs is healthier (it is good for your heart and will firm up your thighs and buttocks). When walking stairs have your key chain ready. *That means in your hand.*
- *When riding an elevator have your key chain in your hand.* Please read chapter five which goes into detail on how to make your weapon and carry it inconspicuously.
- If you are in an elevator and your intuition makes you think there's something funny going on—if the small hairs on the back of your neck come up—*pay heed to your natural instincts. Move close to the person you feel is a threat.* If he is across the elevator from you, it is more difficult to   99

HOW TO PROTECT YOURSELF AND SURVIVE

No matter what your age, an attack is always surprising. This is a typical elevator happening.

LEFT: This time the attacker gets the surprise! Our well-prepared senior citizen defends herself.

RIGHT: She leaves—with her handbag. The elevator mugger may never attack another woman.

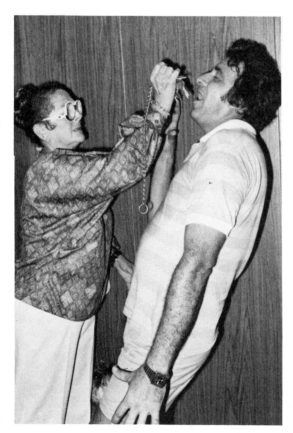

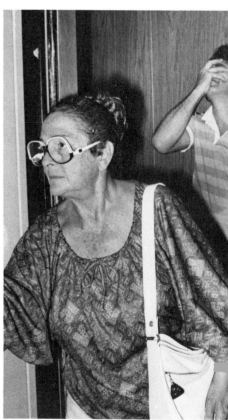

defend yourself. In other words, *if you are alone with a man on an elevator, make sure he is in your striking range.*

- If you feel someone is a threat, do not get off the elevator on an apartment floor because he may follow you and most likely no one will come to your aid. You are better off right in the elevator because it could stop on any floor to admit passengers. A mugger knows this.

As a mental exercise, start imagining an attack by a fellow passenger the next time you ride an elevator. Mentally plan your combination with your key chain. Imagine the worst. In that way, should your fantasy ever become reality, you will be able to deal with it. If you study striking points, each elevator ride you take from now on will be educational. No one will know what you are doing because you will, of course, keep an impassive face throughout this mental workout.

The one time you are not prepared, the time your key chain is buried deep in your bag instead of being in your hand, is the time you are likely to have a problem.

In an elevator be aware. Should someone try to attack you, attack them! You will really have to hurt an attacker in an elevator. You are stuck in there with him and cannot run away. I would suggest continuing to strike until the attacker loses consciousness. Get off the elevator and leave him there.

Vestibules, Entranceways, Outside Your Front Door

After elevators these are the most likely places to be attacked in. Five P.M. to seven P.M. is the most dangerous time. Muggers wait for people to come home from work. Most of the women I spoke to who were held up at this time of day were carrying packages of groceries. Maybe the mugger spotted them in a market and followed them home. Who knows? But if you are carrying bags of food, be aware of those around you and of anyone following you.

LEFT: Your front door is a combat zone.

RIGHT: Your key chain will get you out of danger.

Before you place the key in your lock (if it's a house and you're outside) look around; make sure you are alone. If you live in a building where you have to walk through two doors to get into the hallway, watch out. That small space between an outside and an inside door is very dangerous and may conceal an assailant. If you think there is someone lurking inside your doorway, leave and call the police. If you're mistaken, if there's no one there, it's still better than looking for yourself. Have your key chain in your hand even after you open the front door. Many an unwary woman has come home to find an intruder *inside* the house waiting. A desperate person will go to any means to obtain funds. My dentist's receptionist told me this story:

She arrived home on a winter's evening after work. She was carrying groceries. She entered the vestibule of her building. Two men who were obviously addicts were waiting for anyone who came in. They knocked her against the wall and demanded her money. She truthfully told them she had only two dollars on her person. They beat her unmercifully *for not* having money on her.

A student of mine had a grim experience in an entranceway: she was walking down a street at night and saw two men ahead of her. Something told her they were up to no good. "My first thoughts were to turn around and go the other way, but I was lazy—that would have meant walking a few blocks out of my way—so I just crossed the street. When I was opposite where they stood, they crossed the street, came to me, and pushed me into a small building entranceway. They had a gun. They took my money, and I thought they were going to leave. Then one decided to have sex—kind of as an afterthought. He told me to get on my knees, and he unzipped his fly and exposed his privates and tried to put them in my mouth. At that point I didn't care if they killed me. I started screaming and crying, and they ran away."

Her mistake was in not paying attention to her intuitive warning. *When your hackles rise, there is something wrong.* Whether or not you believe it, you are an animal capable of smelling adrenaline. An attacker's adrenaline is up and emanating an odor. Maybe this is the cause of your sudden awareness. Pay attention to your own fears. Some fears are self-protecting. Fear of rain makes one use an umbrella; fear of losing produces champions. Develop good, constructive fear reactions. Don't ever be ashamed of being afraid of avoiding a confrontation. Your primary obligation is not to fight but to avoid the fight.

Be careful of building entrances and of *walking by* small building entrances, and always have your weapon ready.

On the Streets in a High Crime Neighborhood

If your job or your residence forces you to walk alone on streets in a high crime neighborhood, it is best to appear part of that neighborhood. Walking with a cocky attitude, a self-confident face, and purposeful stride is body language that says you belong.

Never appear fearful. Darting glances, a tightly clutched handbag, shoulders held high, eyes open wide—all telegraph fear and will bring a mugger right to you. You look like a mark.

Carrying a pocketbook is probably not as necessary as you think. You can cut down on the number of things you carry and use pockets. I do this whenever I have to be in a neighborhood known for street crime. If you have no pocketbook a mugger thinks you're not juicy prey.

Dress down. Don't put on your designer special for a stroll around the neighborhood. Put on your jeans or other casual clothes.

Always have your key chain ready for action.

Banks

Many, many times, I have seen women withdraw cash at a bank and actually hold the dollars in their hands and walk outside the bank before they put the money away. This is a terrible mistake. A desperate person may accost you. Be secretive about your money. If you are picking up a large amount at a bank, insist that you be given the money in private. Forget about using a plain brown paper bag as a disguise for a lot of cash. Almost everyone is aware of that ploy—certainly thieves are. *If you use a cash machine outside a bank,* look around, note who is on the street and watching the cash machine; this is a common place for muggers to pick up a victim.

Do not establish regular patterns for picking up money. Never pick up money at the same time or on the same day of the week. Don't make large cash deposits at the same time on a regular basis. (Small business owners beware.) You never know who is watching you or who will inform a thief of your habits.

I was once in a bank where an officer accompanied me to a teller's window to OK the cashing of a check. The man in front of us in line was picking up cash. The officer whispered to me that the gentleman was wealthy and picked up about ten thousand dollars each day. If I had had a criminal turn of mind that man might have been in trouble. Intentionally or not, the officer could have caused trouble for that bank customer. So don't establish regular patterns with cash deposits or withdrawals.

Fighting Your Way Out of a Parked Car

Cars are often scenes for violent rapes, beatings, and murders.

If it becomes necessary for you to get out of a parked car by force, you must strike into the eyes, throat, and solar plexus of your assailant, using either your empty hand or, better yet, your key chain. You must strike hard and fast, *unlock* the car door, and get out. If you are in a car with an automatic lock, and the controls are only on the driver's side, you will have to tell whoever is forcing you to stay that you are willing to cooperate. Try to make him comfortable; suggest that he sit where he can stretch his legs out. If possible, *get to the driver's side of the car before you strike.* If you can't, you will have to disable your assailant enough to reach across and open that lock. Just make sure you know where the releases for the locks are and plan your moves accordingly. *Do not let him see you looking at the locks.* This is a difficult situation and will call for your total concentration.

*This is
a big mistake.*

*Alert, with
key chain ready.*

*The well-trained
woman stops
the robbery attempt.*

Hitchhiking

Sometimes it is necessary to hitchhike. Be careful if you are hitching. There are some firm rules you should follow:

- Have your key chain in your hand all the time you are in the car! Conceal it in your pocket, or pretend you have a nervous habit, and play with it in the open.
- Try to choose your people. An older couple is a pretty good gamble. A woman alone or with children is a good bet and so is an older man in a business suit.
- Don't get into a car or truck with two men or more.
- Watch out for "wise guys." You can tell if a man is openly leering at you or is too anxious for you to get in the car.

Hotel Rooms

Many of the rapes reported to me happen in first-class resort hotel rooms. Here's one:

Katy and her friend were sharing a room in a hotel on a tropical island. The room had a balcony. A man entered the room in the middle of the night. He was totally crazed, threatened them with a knife, and tried to rape both of them. Katy tried to fight. She had taken Tai Chi Chuan, but the gentle art had not prepared her for this.[1] Somehow, her girl friend got out of the room and ran (Katy hoped for the police). Meanwhile, the man raped Katy and was just on his way out of the window when she heard the police at the door. Enraged and crazy herself, Katy tried to hold the man. She grabbed his arm and tried to pull him back in the window. He cut her with the knife. She let go. He got away.

Another woman was in an expensive suite in the plushest hotel on the same island, which is known for its gambling. She had worn diamonds to the casino and evidently someone within the hotel had tipped off a thief. He broke into her room in the middle of the night and demanded her jewels. She gave them to him; then he raped her. When she called the hotel authorities, she was intimidated. First they insisted that she had invited the man to her room; then they asked if she had insurance on her jewels, implying that this was a scam on her part to bilk an insurance company. She got no sympathy, and the hotel detective openly leered at her, as did the police who arrived later. It was awful.

Hotels are hotbeds of gossip. You might think you are incognito when you are a guest, but that's not true. Many hotel employees are watching you and noting what is of interest to them. If you are in a tourist hotel, watch out! My collection of statistics says you have a good chance of running into trouble. Here are some rules to help you avoid a ruined vacation:

- Purchase a lock in a hardware store and take it with you. You can lock your door from the inside while you sleep.

---

[1]This ancient Chinese martial art is a complete balance and muscular control system, initially designed to maintain, heal, and calm the mind, and to increase longevity. Self defense is included only in advanced Tai Chi training, and it takes years of training to get to the point of practical application.

- If there is a balcony with sliding doors or a window off your room, some one can jump to it from another balcony or from the street. There are ways of jamming beds against sliding doors or pushing dressers against windows. Of course, you should lock your windows and balcony doors, but don't count much on that procedure alone to protect you. If a thief wants to get in he will. You may not want to spend your vacation moving furniture around, but it's a lot better to develop some push-power moving beds and dressers, than to deal with what happens when a stranger enters your room at night.
- Make sure you put your valuables in the hotel safe at night. That includes your cash. Don't bring too much cash with you. You can establish credit with the hotel; carry travelers' checks or use credit cards.
- Be careful about inviting new acquaintances, particularly natives of the country or area you are visiting, to your room. People on vacation tend to be much looser, more social than they would be at home. Get to know something about a new acquaintance; at least get his address. Ask a new friend for his telephone number; tell him you'll give him a ring the next day and make sure he answers that phone. At least you know where he can be reached, and he is less likely to harm you if he knows you can trace him.
- Have a weapon near your hand at night. Your key chain is wonderful, and so is a cannister of tear gas or some ammonia in a spray bottle. (Note: in some states using tear gas is illegal.) You can hook that up yourself. As long as you are inside where there is no wind interference, you should be able to hit a face target with no trouble. (See chapter six on weapons you can make yourself.)

Don't *you* be a statistic. Protect yourself and survive! Learn from your sorry sisters who have had vacation-ruining experiences.

Of course this advice should hold true in any travel accommodation, not just hotels. Wherever you are, make tight security.

Traveling in Foreign Countries

Travel is wonderful, and more and more women are flying around on business trips and holidays to exciting places. Enjoy them, have a good time, and continue to maintain vigilance.

Do not go off to the countryside with a new acquaintance unless you tell the hotel concierge, with your new friend right there, where you can be reached. This way, the man has been seen with you and will be less likely to harm you. Check up on home addresses and telephone numbers just as carefully as you would if you met someone in a singles bar at home.

Do not buy drugs or contraband items, no matter how enticing the offer seems. There are a lot of funny things going on in the world and you don't need to become involved in a deal that could ruin your life. Our American government is negotiating with the Turkish government to obtain the release

of four young American women who have been imprisoned for years because of a small amount of marijuana. Whatever they were doing, I'll bet it wasn't worth the time they've spent in a foreign prison.

I know women who have been approached to carry contraband and offered large amounts of money for what seems like very little work. Don't do it! American jails are palaces compared to lock-ups in other countries.

Watch your passport. Make sure you have your passport number written down somewhere in case it should be lost. Passports are valuable to criminals and bring high prices. Watch yours.

Getting Arrested

Confrontations with police are common. Regardless of the reason, the charge, whether you are guilty or innocent, there is only one way to act: respectfully! You are in their hands and subject to their will at this point. Police brutality is not usually directed at women, but it happens.

One of my students was stopped by the police in a rural area far from home. They were hostile to any strangers, and there was a moment when she thought they might beat or rape her. She heard them discussing it. Whether it was just to scare her or a real possibility, she was in terror. But she was smart. She kept her mouth shut and was totally respectful to the police even though they were not respectful to her. She realized that she was in a very small town, out of her element, and totally helpless.

Luckily she got out of the situation without being harmed. If she had challenged those police officers ("I'll have your jobs for this" or, "You have no right to act this way"), they definitely could have harmed her and no one would have known the difference. She used good judgment.

So, always be 100 percent respectful to police, even if you are cuffed around! There is nothing else to do under the circumstances. The worst thing you can possibly do is antagonize them. You are out of your element—in their waters. Control your hysteria: say; "Yes, Officer" and "No, Officer." Speak quietly; avoid using slang or "hip" expressions; do not respond to goading.

Interrogation and fingerprinting are just routine. This may be an earthshaking experience to you, but the police go through it many times a day. Look at it this way and go along with the routine, knowing you have a right to remain silent and a right to have an attorney's advice before making a statement.

If you are interrogated by the police, tell them nothing. If they are nasty about the questions they are asking you, ask *them* nicely: "Aren't I allowed to speak to a lawyer, before answering questions?" If the going gets rough, try to act stupid but nice. If they think you are very dumb, they will assume they are wasting their time and be more likely to leave you alone. If you have been treated badly, remember the facts. Once you're out of there to safety (released or on bail), you can press charges.

You will be searched, so be prepared. A female officer will examine your person. She may look inside your mouth, your vagina, and your rectum. How far they go with the search is up to them, and may depend on the charge. If **107** they are looking for contraband they will probably do all of these things. This is horrible, but there is nothing you can do. If you resist they will examine you by force and it will be worse. Cooperate.

The Cell and Your Fellow Prisoners

You may be alone in your cell, or you may have company. This is not the best place to make new friends, so stay by yourself. If you try to share cigarettes and details of your personal life, you may find yourself the target of more hardened prisoners. Their resentment of you may provoke both verbal and physical abuse, and you may not be prepared to deal with it. Here are some prison rules:

- Mind your own business.
- Don't ask questions or become familiar with other prisoners.
- Don't accept gifts from other prisoners.
- Don't offer gifts to other prisoners.
- Do not show fear, if threatened. Remain silent, and keep an expressionless face.
- Do not cry.
- If someone hits you or tries to hit you, hit her back with a good, swift combination.
- Do not admit to having any knowledge of the martial arts.
- Stay silent as much as possible.
- Whenever you are alone, do knuckle pushups. This will boost your iron will, give you courage, and show you how strong you really are. It will also give you one hell of a punch. Work on your strike combinations in the air. Work on your techniques in the air at high speed, imagining an opponent in front of you. This must be done secretly. Martial arts are against prison laws. If you cannot work out physically, *work out in your mind*. This is an effective alternative. Just practice everything in your mind and accompany this mental workout with the name of each technique. See the combinations in your mind's eye. Your martial arts will sustain you in an emergency situation such as jail. Use them.
- Say your virtues; they will give you hope.

Now that you know where the combat zones are, act accordingly, and *don't be caught on the battlefield without a weapon.* Be aware, keep alert, and you'll make it through without being wounded in action.

HIGH HEELED SHOES

Women wear a disadvantage on their feet—high heeled shoes. They are precarious at best, but for fighting they are terrible. Granted, you have a weapon at the end of your heel, *if you can apply it.*

Your balance is off when you are wearing high heels. That is why you see pictures in this book of students practicing in different types of shoes. You must do the same thing! Get used to high fashion shoes in case you have to defend yourself while wearing them.

The basic rule would be to use only your hands. Don't take the chance of falling when fighting. You would probably hurt yourself and give your attacker a terrific advantage. *Don't try to kick your shoes off.* There is no time for that.

I was riding in a taxicab in a big city. The driver was insane—ranting and raving, driving in erratic patterns. He was calling me names. When he stopped at a red light, I climbed out and started walking across the street. It was winter, and there were piles of frozen snow on the sidewalk. I had on high heeled boots. My awareness button was "on," and I heard him running after me. I turned to face him. I realized I was on icy, uneven terrain, in heels. It was a bad moment, because just walking on that surface without falling required all one's concentration.

I committed myself to hand fighting. I saw by the way he bunched his fist and held his arm that his punch would come around. I mentally prepared to block and strike at the same time. He was cursing very loudly. I sensed a lot of people around—watching. No one intervened. I just settled and waited. All of a sudden, he said: "What, do you know karate or something?" I said nothing. My hands were not high in a fighting position (I did not want to telegraph my defenses), but the way I was waiting for him, with obvious concentration, must have tipped him to something strange. Still ranting and swearing, he backed off and returned to his cab, which he had left right in the middle of a main street.

Practice your self-defense in all types of shoes and barefoot. *Also, do combinations of hand techniques only* in case you cannot use your feet. Conversely, I would suggest doing some *leg and foot combinations only,* left hand combinations only, right hand combinations only, left leg and foot combinations only, right leg and foot combinations only.

You must be prepared for *all* emergencies and able to defend yourself with only one limb. Try approaching a trapped cat with one limb free. Think of that premise.

I'm not going to stop wearing high heels because of my experience, and I don't expect you to either. Just be able to function with them on, and understand the disadvantage of wearing them.

IT REALLY HAPPENS!

Getting Knocked Down

It is possible to be walking down the street one moment, thinking about what you're to wear to the party, and wham—you're hit. Down you go; everything is a blur; you can't see clearly. You're on the ground, and whoever knocked you down is coming toward you.

The specific techniques to be applied here are taught in chapter three (in the heel striking section). Knowing how to fight from the ground gives you a great advantage, and these techniques will stop any further harm from coming to you.

The most important thing for you to do is pull yourself out of the haze; you must force yourself to see your target and defend yourself. This requires iron will. You can faint later, after you protect yourself. No bravado is required on your part—just the opposite. Do not telegraph that you are going to fight. It is good to lie still, pretending that you are knocked out. You can lie on the ground with your leg in chamber and look weak and defenseless. This chambered position on the ground can look very strong, or it can look fetal. The latter will serve your purposes.

If something hurts, you must disregard the feeling and continue to function. Whatever is causing the pain can be fixed later, after you dispense with the attacker. If you give in to discomfort now, it's likely that you will be subjected to a lot more pain or even death.

Don't bother trying to see his face or to search for intent. Just see your striking point—*his knees*—nothing else matters.

Seeing Your Own Blood

Many of the tales of terror recounted to me include bloody incidents, and there is always terrible revulsion on the part of the wounded woman. This usually results in freezing up or fainting. Seeing blood keeps her from functioning in her own behalf.

Get over this squeamishness about blood. It serves no good purpose in your life and only hampers proper reaction under emergency circumstances. If you don't know first aid, take a course. They are available at most schools and given several times a year by the Red Cross. It is necessary to know how to take care of yourself if you get hurt and need immediate attention. It is also important to be able to take care of someone else. Everyone should know how and where to apply a tourniquet.

If you are hurt and bleeding, you must get rid of the attacker who caused the wound and then stop the bleeding. It is stupid to be mesmerized while watching your vital fluids seep away.

The "Giving Up" Feeling

No matter how well-trained you are, how prepared for combat, there may come a time when all seems lost. You may want to give up, feel sure you can't go on defending yourself, positive it's time to meet your fate. No! You *can* go on and on and on.

Here is a slogan that I have adopted. It was given to me by Grand Master Peter Urban and I devoted a whole chapter to it in *Jump Into Shape*. I'm going to pass it on to you and hope that it will boost you out of the "giving up" feeling when you say it to yourself. This slogan hangs in my *dojo*,[2] and you can hang it in any room you work out in. Just glancing at it from time to time can set this never-give-up premise in your mind:

LET'S GO!   KEEP GOING!   THERE IS NOTHING ELSE!

[2]*A dojo* is a temple-gym where martial arts are practiced.

Being Scared out of Your Mind
and Having to Wait for the Opportunity to Strike

This is very likely to happen. It has happened to me several times under different circumstances. You might feel this way if you had been kidnapped and were being held in a room waiting for an abductor to come in. Imagine being trapped at the end of a long alley, watching a threatening attacker walking toward you.

You can't release with a scream at this point, because you're not ready to attack. Besides, a scream would forewarn the assailant.

Breathe. It is that simple. Concentrate on breathing in through your nose and out through your mouth. Don't make a big deal over it and pant out loud. Do it quietly. It will calm you. *Fear tends to make you hold your breath.* You cannot think or function on your own behalf without the proper amount of oxygen reaching your brain. As soon as you *feel* your breath and *hear* your breath inside your body, you will be calm enough to decide your course of action.

Personally, as soon as I calm myself with breathing, I mentally repeat my martial art code and commit myself to my fate: "The martial arts are my secret, I bear no arms. May God help me if I ever have to use my art."

Think something to help calm your mind now that your breathing is under control. If you believe in a spiritual being, now is the time to call. It is good to have help when going into battle. Soldiers pray before battle for good reason. Whether to an emperor, an ancestor, or a god, it helps.

Believe it or not, a joke can work. If you have a turn to humor, cracking an inside joke to yourself can pull you back to the reality of dealing with the situation at hand. This method has worked for a few women I know.

Whatever it takes, you must pull yourself together. Remain calm to think! It is difficult. If you become hysterical and give in to the moment, you will be lost.

I have spoken to a lot of professional fighters. They all say the worst moments occur while waiting to get into the ring. Once in, everything goes right along, and there is no time for thinking. Everyone is scared before a fight; you will be too. Prepare for that moment and train for it, just as you do for the actual physical contact.

The Moment of Truth

That moment when you act in your own defense for the first time, in a real situation, must be one of clear thinking. That's the only way you can possibly survive and overcome your attacker. Actually facing an attacker and dealing with his onslaught is different from practicing self-defense alone or with a partner—very different. Only the serious student who has concentrated on perfection of form and discipline will succeed. Let it be you! There are two ways the moment of truth can occur. Let's examine them.

The Sudden Attack

A grab from behind may be the only indication that something is wrong. In this case, you will let fly with your back-grab combination. The same would apply to a quick side grab or an unexpected grab at your throat from the front. (See chapters four and five for empty-hand and weapons combinations.)

It is actually easier to deal with a sudden attack because you have no time to consider your actions and are likely to act as trained. You don't have to worry about panic because it's all over before you know it.

The Attack with Warning

Sometimes you know in advance that you are going to have to defend yourself. For instance someone may be threatening, cursing, and waving fists around when you can't get away or someone may be trying to rape you. *If an enemy approaches, forget about yourself.* "The consciousness of self is the greatest hindrance to the proper execution of all physical action," according to Grand Master Bruce Lee, *Tao of Jeet Kune Do.*

You must observe only your opponent and what *he* is doing. Know where on *his* body you will strike. There is nothing else. What you are afraid of does not matter now. Unless you act, it will happen.

See. See the places you are going to strike, nothing else. It is easy to see a whole figure while looking straight ahead. Do not telegraph that you are checking out the vulnerable areas of your attacker's body. If you look at his knees, then his groin, and so on up his body, he doesn't need to be a genius to guess what you're planning. Your moment of truth may be upon you. As Bruce Lee says, "An excellent moment to launch an attack is *when the opponent is preparing an attack. His intention and hand movements will then be momentarily concentrated more on attack than defense.*"

The first step: *100 percent commitment to your task.*

The second step: *Logical planning of your strikes.* Remain calm within the moment of terror. It is time to be tactical, practical, and deadly.

The third step: *Execution of a combination suited to the position of the attacking body.* There is no personality now, only an object to be dispensed with. So, to stop the butterflies that race through your stomach and the shakes that want to grab you, let the adrenaline out *now. Move forward, screaming and striking.*

Whatever you do, make sure it is strong and aimed through the body. *Now* is the time to blast that palm heel strike to the base of the skull. How? *Through the front of the face.* If you use your powerful knees or elbows, the same rules apply. *Strike through* and you will succeed. Never be tentative. Take the commitment you made and use it well. There is no time to think about form, particulars of technique, chambers, etc. You're prepared: just throw the strikes. This is the moment you trained for.

After the Moment of Truth

Once you get to safety after defending yourself for the first time, you may break down. That's expected. Give in to the feelings, and let your emotion out. I have seen winning fighters come down with shakes that lasted for fifteen minutes after a bout.

After your initial reaction there will come a feeling of pride and exhilaration. After all, you did it! This is good and you may be justly proud of yourself. *Don't get carried away with this feeling.* Over confidence can ruin you! Remain humble and thank your maker for being alive.

I have seen women who have successfully defended themselves once become like sharks who have tasted blood. They believe they are infallible and subsequently let down their protective guard. Don't.

You have a war story now. Tell it to other women in hopes it will give them the incentive to learn to defend themselves.

Do not stop training because your self-defense worked for you. You must keep up your practice of the martial arts or you will lose your capacity for spontaneous action.

Congratulations!

EIGHT The All-American Crime: Rape

Theoretically, if everyone were trained in the martial arts from childhood, rape as we know it would probably not exist anymore—
Grand Master Peter Urban

It is possible to stop rape.

I'm not going to shoot statistics at you; they're hard to read. If you want them, go to your local precinct, or read the books on rape listed in the suggested reading list of this book. The figures will astound you. They astounded me.

Rape is so common that you are more likely to get raped than not in your lifetime! And besides what's on the books, I have my own information gathered from women across this country—stories that will never be brought to the attention of the authorities.

I'll bet you, from one woman to another, that something has happened to you in your life—a crime against you which you didn't report. Am I right? Well, it's the same with your sisters. No one talks about it—it's the shameful secret we bear in our weakness. Yes, our weakness, our physical inability to stop assaults upon our persons.

If you look back at history, rape has always been the sport of invading armies. You will find no society or era that existed without rape. In Susan Brownmiller's *Against Our Will*, she spells it all out. Reading her book made me decide to die rather than submit to such atrocities. I would suggest you read it, too.

Authorities say only ten percent of rapes are ever reported. I personally think it's less than that. What's the use? If, God forbid, you are raped and call the police, the experience of reporting the whole thing (the innuendos, the sly looks, the disbelief on the officer's face) can be worse than the physical rape. And the trial, the public exposure, can debilitate you for life!

Men like to rape. I remember overhearing a conversation between two established businessmen who had been officers in the Korean War. They did not know I could hear them, and they were actually talking about how much fun it was to kill and rape in wartime! Rape has always been accepted by our society as one of those "little things" that happen. *But no man ever raped a woman who knew how to fight.*

114 Medical evidence of rape now given in court leans heavily on the presence or absence of sperm in the victim. *Viva* magazine ran an article on rape, and one of the leads read: "If you were alone, didn't physically struggle, and he wore a condom, you can practically forget about prosecution."

Changing the rape laws is very difficult. It's easier to work to stop rape. Fight! Don't be a sitting duck for any guy that gets the urge. Fight!

> *In my self-defense class. . . . How strange it was to hear for the first time in my life that women could fight back, 'should' fight back and make full use of a natural advantage; that it is in our interest to know how to do it. . . . Fighting back. On a multiplicity of levels, that is the activity we must engage in, together, if we—women—are to redress the imbalance and rid ourselves and men of the ideology of rape.* —Susan Brownmiller, *Against Our Will*

In December, 1975, I gave a Women's Self-defense Day. It was held at the Universalist Church in New York City. Five hundred women came to be trained! They were terrific—from every walk of life, from teens to grandmas. They were all there—yelling, learning to get out of a front choke, and swinging key chains with fury. Every TV network news program picked up the event.

That night as I sat exhausted watching my students on television, I was appalled that one network chose to follow-up with an "expert" who was questioned on the subject of women's self-defense. "Our studies show," said the woman, a volunteer police worker, "that it is better for women not to fight back. They are more likely to be harmed."

There was no mention of whether those women were trained and able to fight back—just a general "Women shouldn't fight." I was roaring mad! Of course, people who don't know how to fight shouldn't! The whole point, the aim of my whole exhausting day, was to teach women *how* to fight back. *So don't listen to people who tell you you'll get hurt if you fight back.* It's not true. If you are properly trained it is the person who is trying to hurt you who will feel the pain.

THE UNARMED RAPIST

First, let's discuss the unarmed rapist. Everywhere I go, whenever self-defense is the subject, women tell me their stories. I listen carefully to each one, evaluating and planning defense moves in my mind. And most cases of rape reported to me are accomplished without a weapon. If a weapon is held by a rapist, he usually puts it down during the actual act, certain of his victim's compliance and fear. And there are many strike combinations you can use to hurt an unarmed rapist.

Let's look at the actual physical positioning of a man's body when he is attempting the act of rape. He must open his pants. If his pants are already open, or off, he still has to deal with your clothing. He must get your underclothing off. *This means he is in your striking range.* If he terrorizes you into taking off your own clothes, he still has to come close in order to indulge in actual sexual intercourse. *Therefore, he is in your striking range.*

There is no more vulnerable position than a man atop a woman about to engage in sexual intercourse. Here is how you are to proceed:

Show weakness. Plead, "Please don't hurt me; I'll do anything you want." Look scared. Wait until he is very close. Then *finger jab to his eyes with all the focus and power you have developed. Strike through to the back of his skull* Then *hightail it out of there.* If you feel that he has you jammed up so that you cannot execute your jab, then *use your thumbs. Push them with all your might into his eyes. Then run.*

It doesn't matter if his eyes are closed. It will hurt him just as much. Close your own eyes, and poke them a bit with your finger. Imagine a full thrust. No one could take it. The eyes are too delicate.

You never know when someone is watching you.

Rape can be stopped.

Flee to safety.

Do not attempt to grab the groin area of a man on top of you. This is what a rapist expects a woman to do in self-defense. You must do the unexpected.

The only time to strike into the groin area is if the attacker is standing over you, and you are lying on your back on the ground. From this position you can strike hard with your heel to the groin, then to his knee, and run. Or *if he is standing in front of you with his legs apart,* you can use a knee strike to the groin, accompanied by finger jabbing to the eyes. Then—run! You have a lot of devastating techniques at your command, *if* you have practiced what I have taught you in this book. Any one of the strikes you have learned will work for you in a rape situation. You know *where* to strike and *how* to strike. You know what the opening looks like. Remember your virtue: *I shall be quick to seize opportunity.* Now is the time.

The single most important thing you have to do is put the rapist at ease. This is probably not the first time he has raped. He will expect his victim to be in terror, a scared rabbit. Go along with that. Cry. Assure him that you just want to get it over with, and let him come close—into his destruction! Don't forget your elbows. They are devastating and a terrific close-range weapon. Think about how many ways you have learned to use them. If you have truly practiced all the techniques in this book, done your repetitions faithfully, you are prepared to defend yourself against rape!

THE RAPIST WITH A WEAPON

He's not too common, but he might show up on your doorstep. Get him to put the weapon down! Again, tell him you won't fight. "Please don't hurt me, I won't scream," are words of comfort to this maniac.

117

Even if he has a knife in his hand during the lead-up, it is very hard for him to hold it at your throat during penetration. If you are forced to let it go this far, he may put the knife aside once he penetrates you. Wait for that moment. Then jab into his eyes, and run. Remember, just because he is raping you does not mean he will leave you unharmed when he is through with the sexual act. He may hate women to the point of raping and then murdering them. He may be a convicted criminal on parole; your testimony might put him away for life. There is *no* way for you to know that he is *just* going to rape you. So, even though there has been penetration, it is not over. Seize your opportunity and strike! You are trained; you can do it.

Use any ruse you have to. If you have been penetrated, moan, show pleasure, anything to provide you with the opening you need.

PREVENTIVE RAPE

> As for preventing rape, there are a number of options there too. You could lead a hermit's existence of life in a cloister...there is a second option. You might take a very good self-defense course and work on becoming strong, healthy, and skilled in karate and street fighting. You'd have more confidence and be able to think more clearly in any situation. You would still have to be careful, but your life wouldn't be as restricted as it is now...in most cases it will give you the necessary edge to properly defend yourself. —Susan Griffin, "Rape: The All-American Crime," Ramparts

Whatever you do, however you do it, fight! Do not allow rape. It is up to each woman to stop rape! Train your daughter, teach other women, make it impossible for rape to happen. Can you imagine Wonder Woman being raped? You can be a modern-day Amazon equipped to handle anyone who wants to accost you.

I call my self-defense courses "Wonder Woman School." With such a strong, female image in front of them, my students can envision themselves as fighting females—especially the youngsters.

Organize groups of women—co-workers, friends—and train together. I have been invited by many companies to train large groups of female employees. I will come to your town. There are martial art schools in your town that offer self-defense courses. Induce your company to sponsor instruction. Persevere. You can make it happen. Fighting back is simply a learned skill like any other.

Large companies offer adult education programs. Let your boss know you are interested in self-defense training if you work for one of these companies. The adult education programs across the country offer all sorts of unusual and useful knowledge. I have traveled across country to teach jump rope classes, but when I offered to teach self-defense, the males who headed the programs in many of these companies balked. You can change things! Let it be known that you want this knowledge.[1] Remember, knowing how to fight still leaves the choice to you. Learning how to fight a rapist does not mean you *have* to. If at the moment of truth you decide to knuckle under, that's your choice. I just want to be assured that you have the options—the knowledge to stop this thing called rape!

As far as doing harm to the rapist, I can only tell you how I feel since we are all different. If I killed someone who was trying to rape me, my thought would be that it was his time to die. I would have no guilt feelings, only the sense of having been a tool of destiny. I would not report the incident. Of course I am speaking theoretically. Since I would leave the area immediately after defending myself, I wouldn't know how much harm I had done.

If the moment comes when you must defend yourself against rape, it is only fear that could stop you from functioning—the physical fear that women have of men. Well, if you have trained, you have an equalizer. That fear will be removed and you will function and not allow this travesty upon your person.

"FRIENDLY" RAPE

The "friendly" rape is scary because it's sneaky. Since it is committed by someone she already knows, a woman may not believe it's going to happen until it is a *fait accompli*. Often the man will then apologize and say he doesn't know how it happened. But it still happened, and he did it. He will probably try to retain his place as a friend. She may not want to see him again, but he's not going to admit to having done anything really wrong. If she calls it rape—his act of "being carried away for the moment"—he will call her crazy. Here are some actual encounters that were related to me by victims of "friendly" rape. It is typical of the jam a woman can find herself in.

Mary G. told me this story:

"My best friend had to go home to take care of an ailing father. She was worried about her husband who was studying for a law exam. He had no time to cook meals for himself and was burning the midnight candles in order to be prepared for his test.

"We had all been friends for a few years. I told her not to worry. I would have Nelson over for dinner. (We lived next door to each other.)

"Nelson came for dinner two different nights, thanked me, and went back to study. The third night he lingered afterward. We were sitting on the sofa. Nelson reached for me, went to kiss me. I told him "no," that we couldn't do this. He just kept pressing me back on the couch all the time I was saying "no." Before I knew it, all his weight was on me. I couldn't move. Then he raped me!

"When it was over, he tried to kid me about it: 'C'mon it's not that serious. You're acting like it's the end of the earth. Betty (his wife) will never know, unless you tell her.' The whole thing made me feel awful. I couldn't tell Betty; it would hurt her too much. I had been used and couldn't do anything about it. If

[1]Write to me in care of GRANT, 401 East 74th Street, Suite 4C, New York, New York 10021. **119**

I called the police both Betty and I would be embarrassed. The end result was that I stopped being close to Betty because I didn't want to be around Nelson."

Sixteen-year-old Cindy related this tale:

"My mother remarried and I thought Steve was the perfect father. He was so nice to me, buying new stuff for my room and going to PTA meetings at school. I really felt great about my home life. Then one night my mom was out shopping, and Steve came into my room when I was changing clothes. I tried to cover myself, but he got this real strange look on his face and grabbed me. I pleaded with him to stop, but he said he couldn't. He put me on the bed and raped me. There was a moment when I saw my rat-tail comb lying close to my hand. I flashed on grabbing it and sticking it in his eye, but then I just couldn't do it.

"After it was all over, Steve got down on his knees and begged me to forgive him. I told him OK. What could I do? Now he's super-nice to me again, buying me things and interested in my school work, just like it never happened. Everytime I see my mother and Steve together, that's all I can think about. I try to avoid him, and I leave my house whenever my mother does so that I don't have to be alone with him. If my mother ever knew what happened she'd probably commit suicide."

Laura told me this story:

"I was a house guest of my best friend, Kathy. We hadn't seen each other for four years, and I had come from Florida specifically to see her. She had married recently, and her letters had raved about her marriage and her wonderful husband. I was ensconced in the guest room and having a great visit. Kathy's husband, Larry, was very nice to me and went out of his way to drive us around town for shopping and evenings out.

"The second week I was there, Larry came into my room in the middle of the night. I woke up with him in bed next to me.

"I tried to push him away. He had his hand over my mouth and he said: 'I'm going to take my hand away, then you can scream if you want to. Kathy is right in the next room.' Then he took his hand off my mouth.

"I didn't scream. I just couldn't. He knew that. I begged and pleaded, but he raped me, all the time telling me that I was enjoying it, that I wanted this to happen.

"The next morning, there he was sitting at the breakfast table. He was grinning away, being nice-as-pie to me, like nothing happened, or we had a special secret.

"I shortened my visit, pleading a sick relative and left the next day. I hate him to this day, but I have never told my friend and never will. She thinks the sun rises and shines for him. If she knew what happened it would destroy her marriage."

Dolly told me this tale of harassment:

120   "I came from Jamaica to work for a family—watch their children and keep the house. I got the job through an agency, and it seemed just what I had wanted.

"One day the wife was out. I was cleaning in the living room and the husband came up behind me, lifted my skirts, and started fooling around with me. He backed me into a corner and pushed me down on the couch. I begged him to stop. He just laughed and told me I'd better be quiet, or he would tell his wife that I had been playing up to him, and then I would lose my job. I really needed the job. I was so scared—I went along with him. I stayed there for two years and whenever he could get alone with me, the same thing would happen.

"The really bad thing was that the lady was so nice to me. Whenever we were alone, she would talk about her husband and what a good man he was. It was terrible."

The stories go on and on—I have hundreds of them, and they all have certain things in common.

- The woman says "no"; the man persists; then the woman *pleads* for him to stop.
- There is always someone the woman does not want to know about the experience; the man is well aware of this.
- The man usually tells the woman that *she* is enjoying what is happening, or that he knows this is what *she* really wanted.
- The man either *jokes about it afterward*, making very light of it, calling it a "lost moment" or "losing his head," or *begs for forgiveness* using the same lines about being carried away.
- *The man does not believe he has done any wrong.* He acts just as he always did before the "friendly" rape occurred and expects the same behavior from his victim. Many times he considers her a co-conspirator.
- *The man considers the first time a beginning* and will continue along these lines whenever the opportunity arises.

OK. So we know that this phenomenon, "friendly" rape, exists. If it hasn't happened to you, there's a good chance that you may have to deal with it one day.

I've got news for you. You can stop it!

Why it occurs I don't really know. Maybe nature calls men in a strong way and the urge to reproduce is beyond their control. Whatever the reason, it will not change things. Accept what is and deal with it. It's up to you to stop a "friendly" rape. If it occurs, it is your fault.

How to Cope with "Friendly" Rape

Let's start from step one: the minute your "friend" tries to touch you, the very second he does the unusual—whatever is against your will—you must say a firm, strong, decisive "no," and push his hand away. Or get up and put space between you and him. Then, without smiling or trying to be nice, tell him to leave. Don't be nasty about it. Just be firm. This is the thing to do if he even

121

suggests sex verbally. A firm "no;" then, "You have to leave now." It's important not to make excuses about requesting his departure. If you do, if you smile or apologize for not wanting to go along with him, he will take that as weakness and try harder.

Step two: if the "no" doesn't work—if you're being pressed physically—it is time for you to become physical in a very specialized way. You have to hit him, bring him to his senses, and leave him his self-respect, all at the same time. A palm heel to his breathing system is perfect. (See chapter three for palm heel striking instructions.) A good swift palm heel to his solar plexus accompanied by a firm "no" will stop him. I'll tell you why: his breathing will be knocked out of him for a moment. That alone will cool him down. But the important thing is that you've shown strength in a manly way! Men hit each other in the chest. A man will have instant respect for a good chest shot. He may even laugh and thank you for bringing him around. He may say; "Wow, where did you learn to hit like that?" He will be surprised. He will not know how many other tricks you have up your sleeve. He will respect you.

The other technique that is acceptable is to be used when he is standing up. It is shove shock[2] described in chapter three. This is accomplished by two palm heels delivered quickly to his shoulders, knocking him backward (probably off his feet) and accompanied by a firm "no." This sudden shoving and shocking will also bring him to his senses and leave him with his self-respect.

Whether you use a palm heel to the chest (breathing system—solar plexus) or the shove shock, don't laugh with him if he finds it funny. *Firmly* tell him to leave. I don't care how you say it: "OK, Buddy, time to go home," or "It's best for you to leave now," or "There is the front door, I would suggest your using it now." I repeat: *firmly* tell him to leave. *Do not apologize*. For example; "I'm sorry, but you'd better go home," or "I didn't mean to hurt you, but you have to go home," are both weak statements. He will sense guilt on your part for hitting him, and he will try harder and probably overcome you. *Do not show weakness.* It is also important *not to make excuses* for asking him to leave, e.g., "I have to go to sleep now; you should leave." That is another sign of weakness. Tell him *firmly* to leave!

If he wants to apologize, to talk it over, to try and make everything right, don't go for that either. Now is not the time. The atmosphere is sexually charged. He has to cool down, so don't spend any time talking over the situation with him. You must get him out of there *now*. A good answer is: "There's no problem, just go home now."—said without a smile. That way he knows that you're not uptight over the situation, just done with it!

Actually, there is nothing to be uptight over. This is a common happening; you've just avoided it; end of story. Don't make a big deal about it. Ranting and raving at him will bring him back on you. He may think that you're going to tell

[2]Shove shock is a specialty that Grand Master Peter Urban teaches only to women. He developed it especially for women and says that all his male students are jealous of this wonderful technique that the women use so well.

the person you both know about it and therefore will want to complete the act so you will have something to hide. Ranting and raving may further stimulate him. So show no passion, please. Just a good firm "no" accompanied by the palm heel to the chest or shove shock.

I have used these techniques in a "friendly" rape situation, and they have worked. Students of mine have used them. Every time the man was left with his self-respect and a hell of a lot of respect for the woman.

Later, the next day, or at the next meeting, these things can be discussed if *you* want to. The man will still be your friend, and you'll find you won't resent him.

If the palm heels don't work (this is rare, but all things are possible and you must be prepared), you are in a self-defense situation, and you will have to hurt him, just as if he were a complete stranger. Don't use a chest strike or shove shock because he already knows about them. You will have to go for broke and deliver a groin strike or a center face strike. If he's raving mad (unusual, but it could happen), you will have to go all out and finger jab to the eyes or kick his knees.

So, after the initial strike and the "no," if he indicates by movement that he's going to hit you, be prepared and strike wisely. Watch him closely, so you know exactly what's happening. Don't turn your back on him—*stay fully aware until he is out of your house.* If you are in his home, leave instantly.

No-Nos for Dealing with "Friendly" Rape

I have talked to a lot of women about "friendly" rape and asked them what they would do under the circumstances. Many of their suggestions would actually harm them, and I will share with you a list of common mistakes.

Face slapping. A lot of the women I questioned came up with an immediate, "I'd slap his face." This is a bad move. First, a face slap is a classical insult and an invitation to fight. In addition to being sexually aroused, he will now be angry. Second, a face slap is not a strong enough technique to make him think you can fight; it will instead show him that you are weak.

Penis slapping. Quite a few women gave this as an answer. Kind of a "cutting-off-the-source" type solution. I don't think so. I think this would be sexually stimulating and make him more aggressive. Again, a slap is not enough if you mean business. A valid groin strike is meant to penetrate through the pelvic structure. A slap means nothing. Don't do it.

Threatening. "I'd tell him I'd inform our mutual friend" or "I'd tell him I'd have him indicted." He won't believe you, not even if you really mean it. It won't stop him.

Pleading and begging. There were a lot of women who felt they could appeal to his sympathies, to his chivalry. Forget it. This is weakness. He will take it as such and advance on his path even more strongly.

Joking. "Oh, no problem—I have a way with men; I'd joke the whole situation away." I don't believe so. This attitude would only make the "friendly" rape more friendly.

123

So, when dealing with "friendly" rape, make a total commitment to yourself to go all the way with self-defense, or don't start. Trust your martial arts. They work.

Grand Master Bruce Lee put it beautifully when he said; "Action is a high road to self-confidence and esteem."[3]

[3]Bruce Lee, *Tao of Jeet Kune Do.*

Living Alone and Loving It

NINE

A female Mockingbird cannot sing unless she has a home of her own.
—Robert Ardrey, *The Territorial Imperative*

More and more women are maintaining their own residences or are active heads-of-households. Tasks and responsibilities once considered for men only are being handled with ease by women. They are plumbing and wiring and dealing with mortgages and repairing cars. But there is one area that is not being properly covered: the protection of the castle and its inhabitants.

If you've taken over all other responsibilities, you should shoulder this one, too. You'll sleep easier in a home with good security and be a lot safer. You are a territorial female now. Let's take a look at your abode and see how secure it is.

WHO HAS YOUR KEYS?

How many people have you loaned or given your keys to so they could run in and pick something up for you? Babysitters? Apartment workers? Building superintendent? Have your keys been left for telephone installers then returned to the building doorman? Have you left your keys with trusted neighbors to admit workmen? How about houseguests?

If any of the above apply to you, change your locks.

What the heck—it won't cost that much and is an absolute necessity as a first step in establishing total security. Don't waste time wondering. Don't justify delay by reestablishing your firm faith in whoever has had your keys. Leave nothing to chance. Start all over. *Change your locks.*

Now that you have new locks, here are some "don'ts" that will keep you safe.

1. If you live in an apartment building *don't leave the keys to your apartment with building personnel.* (I know that many buildings have rules that say you must, but you can avoid it.) Leave a bogus key, or say you're having one made up, when they remind you that they don't have a key. Or leave only the key to the bottom lock, (and always lock both top and bottom so no one can get in anyway). After all, if there's a fire in the building you can bet no one **125**

is going to try to save your valuables. They will get out of there and save their own lives.

2.   Your extra set of keys should be left with one person or in one place where you can always get to them should you lose yours. Mothers are a good choice; best friends are often willing. If you have property you can bury the extra set. (Make sure no one observes you.) But please, *have only one extra set. Don't start passing out keys again.*

3.   If you have school children and they have to come in and out when you're not there, *make necklaces with strong chains and have them wear the keys. Don't let kids carry house keys unless they are around their necks tucked inside their clothes.*

4.   *Don't ever give top and bottom lock keys to anyone.* For instance, if you have a babysitter who needs to use a key, give her the bottom key only. She can lock both top and bottom from the inside for security. When she leaves just have her lock whichever is the stronger. *Always use the same key for this purpose.* That way, even if someone has it copied, it won't give them access.

GENERAL HOUSE SECURITY

Call your local police department, and ask to have someone check your house for security. They will be glad to do it. An officer will come to your home and go over doors and windows and evaluate your locks and security with you. Take the advice given even if it's a bit troublesome to follow. It is a lot more trouble to replace everything you own or to come home and find a stranger in your house.

If you live in an apartment with a terrace, or if there is a fire escape near your window, install wrought-iron bars. I know it's awful to have to do that, but it's still better than unexpected surprises. Some wrought-iron guards come in flower patterns, or you can train ivy to wind around the bars.

Don't succumb to the "I live in a good neighborhood syndrome." That's where the best pickings are! A thief would rather crawl into the window of a beautiful home than a shanty.

Your Front Door

Make sure you have a telescopic peephole in your door so you can see down the apartment hallway or into the front yard; or have a window in your house that affords a clear view of the door and surrounding area. (Women have told me they looked out of a peephole, saw one person, opened the door and then another, who had been hiding down the hall, joined his partner for a forced entry.) Don't be lazy, even if you have to look out of an upstairs window.

If someone has a delivery, and you have to sign for it, let them slip the paper under the door. Sign it, slip it back under the door, and tell them to leave the package outside for you. This is not over-caution. A lot of women who have told me of forced entries into their homes also commented that they wished they had taken this precaution. Let people consider you eccentric. Let delivery men laugh. You be safe; that's what's important.

Don't put a chain on your door and open it. They are flimsy and a strong shoulder can pop them at will.

Repairmen

There are a lot of devices and machinery in your home that will need outside attention at one time or another. No matter how reputable the firm that sends him or how long you have been using their services, don't take your eyes off a repairman. Have a weapon at hand all the time he is in your house. Your key chain is perfect. If he's working in the kitchen, take that time to make phone calls you've been putting off. That way you are in contact with someone and keeping busy so he doesn't notice your attention.

A full third of the rapes that are reported to me[1] are committed by servicemen allowed into the home. Many times they are building repairmen the women have known for years or even superintendents of buildings. There is something about being alone with a woman in her home that makes men rape.

It is a good idea to ask a service establishment what their man looks like and to ask him to pass his identification under the door before he comes in. One sorry woman told this tale: she was expecting a service man to repair pipes. She asked who it was through the door. The man on the other side named the business she had called. She opened the door and admitted him. He robbed and raped her. He might have been in the shop she called and might have overheard the job order; somehow he found out she was expecting a repairman. Be careful.

Where to Keep a Weapon

If you live in the open spaces and keep a gun, it should be within your reach when you are sleeping at night. When you are out of the house, it should be by the front door. That way, if someone forces you to bring him home, you can reach for it as soon as you open your door. Some police departments have regulations that state exactly where guns are supposed to be in a home. Check them out.

Keep your key chain where you can reach it at night. A spray-bottle of ammonia is also a good defense. (See chapter six.) If someone is going to break into your home, it will probably be at night.

YOUR DOG—YOUR BEST FRIEND

I am of the firm opinion that every woman who lives alone should have a large dog as a companion, and the large dog should be attack-trained!

A big dog has a big bark and anyone considering your home as a target will change his mind when Fido lets loose with a few woofs.

---

[1]Women volunteer this information when I am on lecture tours, giving self-defense clinics or counseling for religious organizations, women's groups, etc. They rarely report it to the police because they don't want the publicity.

*A big dog
protects the
front door.*

Anyone who is in your home will be very aware of the dog and mind his P's and Q's. That includes repairmen and dates!

If you have a canine companion, your loneliness will be over (if you're lonely), and a wonderful friend will always be with you.

To you apartment dwellers who say, "It's cruel to keep a dog in an apartment," I disagree. Apartments are fine places for dogs, and that includes big ones. Some large dogs (Great Danes, for example) do not require much exercise; others, such as a Weimaraner I once had, can be taught tricks that can be done right at home and provide all the exercise they need. (Mine learned to jump over a home-made jump thirty times non-stop every day, providing a complete cardiovascular workout.)

Having a dog will also get you out! Walking your dog in a big city is a wonderful way to meet people and make new friends. If you are a sports enthusiast, you will have enthusiastic company. Jogging is more fun with a dog. My dog swims along with me. Even taking a ride in the car is more fun with a dog along, and the dog will also protect your car.

If you have kids, the dog will take care of them in the city. They can walk the animal, get out themselves, and you won't have to worry.

If You Are Afraid of Dogs

If you have a deep-seated fear of dogs (maybe you were bitten as a child, or your parents instilled the fear in you), you can get around that easily. Get a puppy. A baby canine is too adorable to fear and cannot possibly hurt you. As the dog grows, you will be totally familiar with it and love it. You may still be afraid of other dogs but not your own.

128

Training

Your best friend will respond better to training if you acquire him as a puppy. This is when he should be obedience trained—including training to hand signals. Any animal I ever had could be directed silently with a slight move on my part. Any good trainer should be able to accomplish this.

Do not have your dog attack-trained until he or she is two years old. That's how long you're going to have to wait. *Don't* purchase an attack-trained dog. You must raise the pup yourself with a lot of love and good discipline. Then, when the animal reaches that two-year mark of maturity, it is ready to go to work.

Check out the attack trainer carefully. *Do not leave your dog with an attack-trainer*; take part in the training yourself. Then you will have a dog who is ready to protect *you*. And no one will ever know he is attack-trained.

TEN Give Me Your Daughter and Your Mother

A few years ago, after teaching a women's self-defense class in a Manhattan health club, a woman approached me with a small child in tow. She pushed the youngster toward me. "I'd like to give you my daughter," she said. And she did.

That's how I met Totes. At this writing, she's eight years old and proudly wears a green belt in karate that she achieved along with the title of "The Littlest Dragon." She's working on earning her next rank of purple belt. She trains hard and is a wonderful example for my other young students who have to work to keep up with her.

Tote's mother is a college professor, a highly educated woman aware of big city problems that can affect a young girl. She has had the foresight to equip her daughter with many skills, including self-protection. You should do the same for your daughter!

MARTIAL ART TRAINING FOR GIRLS

History shows us that men have always trained their sons to fight at early ages; they recognize that their sons need to know how to protect themselves to survive. Do you know of any other species on this planet that produces a helpless, unprotected female? I don't. Even the gazelle, so delicate and beautiful, is equipped with the speed of lightning for sprinting to safety. Check out a female cat. She is a ferocious fighter, and the first training she gives her young is in how to fight. Gorillas are very close to us, physically and biologically. Males and females do not fight each other, but the female can fight any other creature that threatens her. Why should it be different for the female child? Why should she grow up to be a "sitting duck," a victim? Most young girls are denied the right to learn fighting skills. As long as they are taught to accept physical harm (and that's what's learned if they are not taught to fight back), they will continue to become battered wives, rape victims, perfect candidates for the psychiatrist's couch.

130

*Totes practices
self-defense
with an
adult partner.*

Here are questions that parents ask me about martial art training for young girls. I hope the answers will clear up any misconceptions you might have.

What Physical Difference Will
Martial Arts Make in My Daughter?

Mind-body coordination and dexterity are well developed in the martial art student. First of all, *she'll grow up with an evenly developed body.* Most women have a sad lack of upper-body strength which manifests itself in later life in the form of arthritis, slack upper arms, and a general rounding of the shoulders and back (widow's hump). The exercise in the classes (which include as much stretching as a ballet or yoga program) leads to a supple, firm figure. Push-ups practiced repeatedly make for upper-body strength and fitness. Stamina levels are high; the cardiovascular system of the martial art student is in fine shape. Your daughter will learn how to jog, jump rope, do calisthenics, jump hurdles, and run obstacle courses. She will work her stomach muscles, and keep a tight middle for life.

Your daughter will see better than other females. In the past, eye training has been for boys only. Throwing balls contributed to this, and only recently, with the popularity of tennis, have women begun to see properly. This is the reason women do not automatically block a punch thrown at them. If you throw a punch at a man, he will push it out of the way. If you throw a punch at a woman, she will close her eyes and get hit. Eye training is developed along with blocking systems.

131

Won't Martial Art Training Make My Daughter Tough and Disrepectful at Home?

No. If anything, the child becomes more respectful toward her parents as the result of martial art school. The martial arts originated in Oriental societies where parental respect is practiced religiously. Mother, father, grandparents, and ancestors are revered by the children. Modern day martial art still teaches respect as the first duty of a child. Time and time again I have seen seemingly impossible problems between parent and child solved by martial art instructors.

At What Age Can My Daughter Begin Studying Martial Arts and How Will it Affect Her School Work?

Six is a good age. There are exceptions, but usually a child's concentration span is too short before that. The strong self-discipline that is part of martial art training touches every aspect of life; school work often becomes pleasanter and achievement more satisfying.

What about Relationships with Peers?

If your daughter is going off to a large school, she's going to have to deal with many difficult situations—possibly even gang confrontations. Having self-confidence and knowing how to protect herself will enhance her popularity.

She will meet and make friends in martial art school. They will become her "family" also—the instructor, her *dojo* mother or father, and fellow students, her *dojo* brothers and sisters. She will form lifetime friends among the adults and children she works with.

What about Injuries?

There are no more injuries than any other form of athletics might produce. Sparring guards are used, mouthpieces are required, and the child is prepared with good blocking systems and watchful instructors.

Will My Child Be Able to Defend Herself Against Attack by an Adult?

Most definitely. The smaller a child, the closer she is to groin level, and the easier it is for her to strike and run. A child trained in martial art would teach a menacing adult a lesson he wouldn't forget. The first thing I teach my new students is street self-defense. I arm them with knowledge immediately, so that no one can hurt them.

Won't This Training Make a Young Girl Aware of Things Too Mature in Subject Matter for Her?

I don't think so. Isn't it better to prepare her to protect herself against harmful attack than to leave her unguarded in the jungle? Children always accept the information I give them very matter-of-factly. They learn to defend themselves against child molesters without blinking an eye. It's the parents who get disturbed.

Because of self-defense training, six-year-old Melissa's parents are convinced that she can protect herself from strangers with evil intentions.

Won't Martial Arts Make My Daughter Masculine?

No. Martial art builds the grace of the ballerina with the fighting abilities of the cat. It neither deepens the voice nor builds unsightly, bulging muscles.

How About Her Relationship with Men as She Matures?

They will be full of respect for her. You won't have to worry about her on dates. She will be capable of standing side by side with her mate, an equal partner in life.

To sum it up, I can see no difference between the natural athletic abilities of boys and girls at early stages. It is all a matter of training and exposure.

It is up to you to see that your daughter knows how to protect herself in this dangerous society. As a female she has to live with the statistics. Why not prepare her to deal with them? Remember, fighting is only a *learned skill*. There is no big mystery to it. Because you are unaware, because you did not learn these skills as a child, does not mean that your daughter should be deprived.

TEENAGERS AND SELF-DEFENSE

To the Mother of a Teenager

You've probably laid down rules and regulations for your daughter's conduct outside your home. It is likely that once your child is out of your sight she totally disregards those laws. Whether or not you like the idea doesn't matter. What does matter is her safety. So, rather than lecture, face reality. Have your teenager read this book, particular this section. It may save her life.

I would suggest a good martial art school or self-defense classes for your teenager. Help her to protect herself when you can't be around.

Don't fool yourself and think that your teen is different. She's going to do what her peers do. I have spoken at length to young girls on the subjects covered in this chapter. They are all out-of-bounds according to their parents rules. But the fun of sneaking, of defying, has its own thrilling aspects. This rebellious time of life (remember back?) can be chock full of trouble. So open your own eyes, and help your teen get through the trials and tribulations of growing up.

Dear Teenager

You have your own special problems. The teen years can be a traumatic and confusing time of life. Many of the difficult moments you may run into are self-defense situations. So here is a special section for your needs:

Liquor and Narcotics

These drugs may be offered to you, or worse yet, you may be dosed. In other words, someone may put something in a drink without your knowledge, that will make you unable to function normally. This "someone" is not your friend and may be planning to harm you. If you feel yourself getting "high," get out of there. Get to a phone and call your parents or a friend you can trust—anyone who will get to you immediately.

Don't wait to see how much effect the drug will have. Start to function in your own behalf the second you become aware of a strange feeling: a psychedelic drug, (LSD, mescaline, etc.) can hit quickly. Fight if you have to; don't worry about making a fuss—just *get out of there.*

Understand that if you are drinking liquor you are putting yourself in a precarious position, where it is unlikely that you will be able to function rationally. So, if you feel woozy from wine or liquor, go home. Spend your lunch money on a cab. *Don't take the offer of a ride home from a stranger.* This is not the time to make a new friend.

If you are in a group where everyone is taking a narcotic, and you feel forced to participate to be "one of the guys," *don't*! Instead, *pretend* to take what's offered. Then, when everyone is no longer paying attention to you, leave. They won't realize you didn't join them. Here is a true story that will show you what can happen when you're out of your element:

Bonnie and Sara (my student) went to a discotheque. They were not supposed to be there, they were underage, and it was against their parents' rules. Nevertheless they'd been going to this very sophisticated dance club for a while and felt right at home.

This night they had just ordered drinks at the bar when two men asked them to dance. After they danced, they returned, gulped their drinks down, and stood talking to their dance partners. Sara excused herself and went to the ladies room where she began to feel strange. She was making her way back to the bar when she saw Bonnie being carried out of the club in the arms of the man she'd been dancing with. Bonnie's head was back and her tongue was hanging out of her mouth. Sara ran to the man, grabbed Bonnie, and pulled her out of his arms. By that time, Sara recalls, a blackness was overcoming her, she couldn't see well, and there was a loud ringing in her head. She pinched Bonnie's neck muscle (a painful little trick I had taught her to snap people back to reality) and told her; "You're not sick; it's a drug. We have to get out of here—pull yourself together." And somehow the two of them made it to the street.

Once on the street, Sara was totally blinded and in a state of paranoia. She thought she would be picked up by the police. She turned to a body she sensed standing next to her and pleaded: "We've been give some horrible drug, please get us home!" and gave her address. Luckily the person she spoke to had a kind heart. He got the two girls home. At home, Sara thought she was going insane and Bonnie was in the same shape. One of her sisters was there (her parents were out) and gave both girls some tranquilizers she found. It took four hours for their return to sanity.

Evidently, the dosing was planned. The men who did it, spotted their victims' tender years and thought they had good marks. While the girls were dancing another of the crew must have dosed the drinks. Who knows what they had planned for Bonnie and Sara? I'm sure it wasn't pleasant.

When Sara told me the story, she said if it hadn't been for her martial arts **135** training she never could have made it through the experience: "I said my virtues, *Sensei*, and a couple of times, I heard your voice telling me nothing was impossible."

Of course Sara swore she'd never go to another bar in her life. But that's hindsight.

You should remember that everyone in a bar is there to indulge in drugs. (Liquor is a drug.) Drugs change people and make them do things that would normally be out of character. If you are going to go to discos and bars, keep an eye on those near you. And watch your drink: don't ever give anyone an opportunity to put something in it.

Marijuana Can Be Dosed

Since pot is legal in many parts of the United States and we hope we will see an end to the jailing of young people across this country for smoking it, teens tend to accept any marijuana passed to them as a gesture of good will. Don't!

There is a horrible drug called "hog" or "angel dust." It is an animal tranquilizer (used to subdue the largest of animals: elephants, gorillas, etc.), and smoking a small amount can easily make a human suicidal.

Many teens have been given "joints" with this drug added. Once under the effect, they are incapable of helping themselves and are at the mercy of whoever dosed them. Many young victims of rape have related stories to me that started out: "The last thing I remember was smoking this joint he gave me."

The way to identify this death-dealing drug is by its smell. There is an odor of parsley when the drug is lit. It is very unlike the sweet smell of marijuana. *Trust your senses.* Don't smoke anything that smells the least bit different, no matter what the person who is offering it to you says it is or how well you know him. You don't need the horror trip this drug can induce.

No, You Can't Come in!

There are times when you need to get someone out of your doorway. For instance, you've been on a date and are standing in your open doorway saying goodnight. He wants to come in, and you don't want him to. He tries to push you inside. *Now use shove shock* (see chapter three). Close your door and lock it.

A lot of teens find themselves in this situation when they are babysitting, and a boyfriend wants to come in.

Shove shock is an easy technique to use at the door. It is sudden, very effective, and will cause no major injuries to the recipient.

On Lover's Lane

You fall into the age group most likely to have car trouble. You might be parked in a young man's car, and he wants to advance along a sexual path, and you don't. You probably like this fellow a lot, or you wouldn't be there. So, if he won't stop, the object is to get out of the car and get home without doing **136** him permanent damage.

*If he tries
to push his way in,
use shove shock.*

*It's time
to stop this.*

*Finger jabbing
to the throat
—a perfect
control device.*

138

*Leave the car
and go home.*

First, try a firm "no," and ask him to take you home. If he stops his advances, don't start kissing again. Get the car moving, and you'll probably avoid a major run-in.

If the firm "no" doesn't work, you have to show him you mean business. Use the finger jab to the throat, but in a pressing manner, not in a striking manner. Here as you can see in the pictures, Pearl controls the young Lothario, giving him time to "get a grip" on himself and also making the point that she means business. She then leaves the car. That is the proper finishing move. You can't execute a physical "no" to stop someone from touching you and then stay around. The situation is just going to start all over again, except this time the male will be aware of your technique, and you won't have a successful repeat. Instead, a rape situation could develop.

Always make sure you have some money with you when you go on a date. That way, if you have to get home by yourself, you're prepared.

A Man's Home

. . . is his territory. You don't belong there on a date unless you are prepared to have sexual intercourse with your host. You are deluding yourself if you think anything different. Time and time again, girls tell me they were raped in a man's home even though he promised to take them home after one drink, or they just went there to see something (a painting, the decorations) or to have a quiet place to talk. Many times men have lured young girls with: "I live with my mother, so you don't have to worry about stopping by," only to find out that "mother" just happened to be out when they got there.

Once you're in his house, and the door closes, he's calling the shots.

139

Going to College

More and more colleges have coed dorms. College girls I have spoken to and school statistics point to a high incidence of rape—violent and "friendly." (See chapter eight on "friendly" rape.) I repeatedly hear about the lax security in the dorms and the over-aggressiveness of male students toward female students.

"When you're dating at home" a coed told me, "the fellow knows that even if your parents are out, they're going to be coming back. He'll leave if you ask him to. But when you're at school it's different. You tell a date good-night, and he doesn't want to hear it. The guys are bigger and really pushy. A lot of the girls get raped."

If you're going off to college, arm yourself with self-defense training. You may never have to use it, but you should know how.

It is important to be able to back up a "no!"

DEAR SENIOR CITIZEN

You have as much right to walk the streets safely as anyone else. But there is a problem. You fall into the age group most likely to be attacked on the street. Take it from me, the statistics show you are in constant danger. This can be changed. You have the ability to defend yourself; all you need is training.

Read chapter five and learn to use the key chain! Get one immediately and make sure you also have a whistle on it. You can easily use this effective weapon. You don't need any power, and you don't have to make contact with any part of your body so you don't risk breaking a bone.

I have trained senior citizens in large groups and always found them quicker to learn, with more basic stamina than younger women. Perhaps it's because the older woman is more aware of the threat to her safety or because she has had more problems. Whatever the reason, I always find senior citizens prepared to train with a good attitude.

Over and over again I hear, "I'm afraid to go shopping."

Going to the supermarket is particularly traumatic for you because a mugger knows you need money to make your purchase, and hanging around food stores is good pickings for these monsters.

Going to the Supermarket

- *Don't carry a handbag.* It's like waving a red flag in front of a bull. Since you're aware of danger you are likely to clutch it tightly and, in body language, tell everyone on the street that you have money. Put your money in your pocket.
- *Have your key chain in your hand* even while carrying your groceries home. You can do it. I do. It's easy to bunch up the keys and still hold a paper bag.
- *Don't look around to see if you're being followed.* That will bring a mugger on. If you hear footsteps behind you, be ready! Move to a populated section of the street if possible. If you are alone prepare to

strike with your key chain. If the person passes you innocently, you will have had a mental exercise in self-protection and that is good for you.

- *Delivery boys should be tipped at the market* and told to ring your bell, then leave the packages outside your door.
- *Watch out for young teenage boys in groups.* Alone each is probably a great kid. Together they are dangerous and cannot be reasoned with.

Martial Arts Programs for Seniors

All good martial arts schools have special programs for senior citizens. Many martial arts schools have volunteer escort services for senior citizens.

If you are having a problem in your neighborhood, contact your local martial art center and see what programs are available to help you. You are certain to make some new friends.

Umbrellas make wonderful weapons. It takes a bit of training which any martial art instructor should be able to give you. Take your key chain with you. Show it to the instructor, and show him or her the technique section in this book. The instructor will help you to perfect the techniques. If you belong to a senior citizens' group or center and are having problems and can't get training, contact me through my publisher and I will come and train you.

You do not have to walk in fear. They're your streets too.

To the Handicapped Woman

If you have to use an apparatus to get around (crutches or a cane) you have a terrific weapon in your hands at all times. A little bit of training will show you just what I mean. Try to stop by a local martial art school and see if an interested instructor will work with you. Hit inanimate objects with your aid. Strike a railing or the side of a building. Get used to aiming and hitting what you see.

If you use a walker, you can hang a key chain weapon on a bar, close at hand.

If you are in a wheelchair you can have your chain handy.

Read the section on weapons (chapter six). Get a key chain and practice. You can defend yourself just as easily as anyone else.

My Masters, My Mentors

How one develops within the martial arts depends largely on the quality of instruction received. I have been the luckiest of students. My martial arts studies have been supervised by greatly skilled masters. In this book I have quoted them, and now I want you to meet them. So, here, in alphabetical order, are my teachers past and present:

THOMAS AGERO

Master Agero, from the Philippine Islands, was trained extensively in Okinawan (*Okinawa Te*) styles of martial art. He is a master of weapons and instructs me in the use of the *sai* (my favorite weapon—the three-pronged sword developed by the Chinese to combat the *samurai* sword of the invading Japanese), the *bo staff*, sword, *nunchakas*, and any other martial art weapon I can find. He is amazing in his dexterity with many different weapons. Most martial art weaponry taught these days is for form's sake and not actual combat; Sensei Agero is a rare instructor, because he actually teaches how to fight with the weapons.

The soft-spoken, patient Master Agero is a fountain of knowledge. He can reel off martial arts facts and history with amazing accuracy. He has contributed a great deal to my knowledge of the ancient ways and my martial art library grows under his tutelage.

RONALD DUNCAN

Master Duncan teaches an ancient art called *ninjutsu* (the art of stealth). *Ninjas* were the traditional assassins of the emperor of Japan. These men, clothed in black, could walk unseen through crowds of people, scale walls like human flies, and kill in seconds. Their ways are used to train our special forces to this day.

Master Duncan teaches this art. He is also a *jujitsu* exponent and an incredible whiz at disarming. In his long and fame-filled career, he has been loaned out by our government to train our allies in these arts. Disarming is a ticklish subject and there's a lot of controversy about the exact moves—which will work and which won't. Master Duncan's work!

JASON LAU

A young Master from Hong Kong, Sifu[1] Lau is my *kung fu* instructor. I study the beautiful art of *wing chun* and the *kung fu* sword with him.

Martial arts and acrobatics are part of Master Lau's family tradition; much of his knowledge comes from his mother. He is steeped in the traditions of the ancient martial arts; some of his disciples live with him and serve the temple where he teaches.

Master Lau is also a movie star and appears in Chinese fighting films. His form is perfect and he actually has the ability to stay suspended in air.

Sifu Lau received commendations from the Mayor of New York City for his help during the crime-ridden night of the July, 1977 "blackout" when he and his disciples defended whole blocks of small businesses against gangs of would-be looters. I am proud to be a disciple.

BRUCE LEE

Grand Master Lee did more for the propagation of the martial arts than any other person in modern times. Using the media to show the beauty of the martial arts, Master Lee made many movies.

His writings are masterpieces of philosophy and technique. I study the beautiful art of *Jeet Kune Do* that he brought to life, and I practice his teachings. His spirit lives in me as it does in all martial artists. Whenever I have had difficulty making a point clear, I have gone to his writings and found the perfect answer.

PETER URBAN

Grand Master Urban is a master of speech, philosophy, and humor, as well as karate. His martial arts background and accomplishments are astounding.

As a young serviceman, Grand Master Urban was the first Caucasian to get through the school of Master Yamaguchi[2] in Japan. He earned high degrees and then brought the art of karate to a skeptical American population. He is directly responsible for training most of the top karate champions this country has produced. His system of karate is called "U.S.A. GoJu." His martial art "sons" have spread this style of karate throughout America and Europe and his patch, with its closed fist, is a familiar sight at tournaments around the world.

Known as the "Father of American Karate," Grand Master Urban's fighting proficiency is legendary; he is a full Master and holds the rank of Tenth Dan (there is no higher rank).

Master Urban's book, *The Karate Dojo*, is a masterpiece of simplicity and should be read by anyone contemplating martial art study.

Master Urban was very taken aback by the feminine, I-don't-want-to-hurt-anyone syndrome, and found its existence hard to understand. He gave this martial art "daughter" much encouragement for the future of women in the martial arts. I am a proud member of the U.S.A. GoJu Women's Lodge #0001. I

[1]Instructor (Chinese)

[2]Famous karate master, reputed to have killed wild animals with his martial arts.

hold the rank of Sandan (third-degree black belt) in U.S.A. GoJu Karate, awarded to me by Grand Master Peter Urban.

RON VAN CLIEF

Known internationally as "The Black Dragon," Master Van Clief starred in the series of films by that name. *The Black Dragon, The Revenge of the Black Dragon,* and *The Return of the Black Dragon* were all wonderful showcases of his amazing talents.

A student of Grand Master Peter Urban, Master Van Clief is unique because he has such a wide range of martial art knowledge. His formative years were spent learning different fighting systems in this country. He earned black belts in many styles. His career took him off to the Orient. He was exposed to the Chinese fighting arts which he immediately took to heart and studied. Master Van Clief teaches the best of all he has absorbed. Unlike many masters who will teach only one style, Master Van Clief's Chinese GoJu system encompasses many martial arts and is constantly changing and expanding. Before he was a master (he is an eighth-degree black belt), he was a fighting champion of the first order and ranked in the top ten competitors for many years.

I studied with Master Van Clief for six years. He awarded me my first black belt. I presently hold the rank of Sandan Ho (third degree black belt) in Chinese GoJu. Master Van Clief is poetry in motion, an ebony sculpture with the heart of a lion, and an extraordinary teacher. Whatever sort of teacher I am is due to my training under this stickler for discipline, this seeker of perfection.

There were other wonderful teachers along my martial arts way. I didn't have the opportunity to pause with them for long. I wish I could have. They contributed to my education and therefore to this book. So I would like to thank:

The Obosan, he opened the door
Master Frank Ruiz who instructed me in the art of Nisei GoJu Karate
Sensei Chaka Zulu who instructed me in the art of Nisei GoJu Karate
Sensei Wilfredo Roldan who instructed me in the art of Nisei GoJu Karate (and was my first instructor)
Master William Chen who instructed me in the art of Tai Chi Chuan.

Suggested Reading List

Adams, Andrew. *Ninja: The Invisible Assassins*. Burbank, California: Ohara Publications, 1970.

Ardrey, Robert. *The Territorial Imperative*. New York: Atheneum Press, 1966.

Brownmiller, Susan. *Against Our Will*. New York: Simon & Schuster, 1975.

Chow, David and Spangler, Richard. *Kung Fu History, Philosophy and Technique*. New York: Doubleday and Company, Inc., 1977.

Fong, Leo. *Choy Lay Fut Kung Fu*. Burbank, California: Ohara Publications, 1972.

Griffin, Susan. "Rape: The All-American Crime." *Ramparts,* Sept. 1971, pp. 26–35.

Han, Bong Soo. *Hapkido, Korean Art of Self-Defense*. Burbank, California: Ohara Publications, 1974.

Kong, Bucksam and Ho, Eugene H. *Hung Gar Kung-Fu Chinese Art of Self-Defense.* Burbank, California: Ohara Publications, 1973.

Lee, Bruce. *Tao of Jeet Kune Do*. Burbank, California: Ohara Publications, 1975.

Lee, Douglas. *Tai Chi Chuan the Philosophy of Yin & Yang & Its Applications*. Burbank, California: Ohara Publications, 1976.

Lee, James Yimm. *Wing Chun Kung-Fu*. Burbank, California: Ohara Publications, 1972.

Loeb, Paul. *Paul Loeb's Complete Book of Dog Training*. Prentice-Hall, 1974.

Medea, Andrea and Thompson, Kathleen, *Against Rape*. New York: Farrar, Straus and Giroux, 1974.

Rhee, Jhoon. *Chong-Ji of Tae Kwon Do Hyung*. Burbank, California: Ohara Publications, 1970.

Schafer, Edward H. *Ancient China*. New York: Time-Life Books, 1967.

*Smith, Robert W. *HSING-I Chinese Mind-Body Boxing.* Kodansha International Press, 1974.

Staples, Michael. *White Crane Kung-Fu*. Burbank, California: Ohara Publications, 1973.

Toguchi, Seikichi. *Okinawan GoJu-Ryu*. Burbank, California: Ohara Publications, 1976.

**Urban, Peter. *The Karate Dojo*. Rutland, Vermont: Charles E. Tuttle Co., 1967.

**Available at Honda Association, Inc., 485 Fifth Avenue, New York, N.Y.

Index

Accuracy of strikes, 30, 43, 47, 63, 78, 79
Adrenaline, 6, 11, 20, 75, 78, 91, 102
Advantage, 9, 35, 40, 93, 109
Against Our Will (Brownmiller), 114, 115
Age and self-defense training: children, 13, 130–34; senior citizens, 3–5, 16, 115; teens, 115
Agero, Thomas, Master, 47, 142
Alcohol, 134–36; effects of, 43, 94–95, 135, 136, combined with drugs, 95
Ammonia, *see* Spray bottle weapon
Amphetamines (diet pills), 95
Angel dust, 136; *see also* "Hog"
Anger, 6, 7, 123
Arm: position of, 23, 31, 35, 37, 71, 81, 82; upper, 17, 45, 131
Arrest, 107–08
Arthritis, 17, 131
Attack, 5, 6, 14, 41, 98, 132; in a car, 8, 136–39; in an elevator, 8, 80n2, 99–101; from the front, 8 (*see also* Choke attack); in your home, 8; from the rear, 8, 50, 66–70, 83, 111–12; from the side, 8, 53, 70–74; on the street, 8–9, 140–41; on public transportation, 91–94; verbal (cursing), 8, 90–91, 96, 109
Attacker, 5, 6, 8, 9, 20, 33, 38, 41, 66, 87, 90, 110, 115; delivery/repairman as, 126–28; drugged, 11, 43, 95–96, 102; drunk, 11, 43, 94–95, 96; height/size as factor, 7, 19, 53–54, 56, 62, 75, 96; more than one, 9–11, 26, 79; "nice guy," 96–97; rejected lover as, 97; *see also* Rapist
Awareness, 91, 102, 109, 112, 123

Babysitting, 136
Bad habits, breaking, 18, 63–64
Balance, 22, 36, 38, 39, 57, 64, 67, 76, 95, 105n1, 108
Balcony/terrace, entry from, 105, 106, 126
Banks as danger zones, 103, 104
Barbiturates (sleeping pills), 95
Battered wives, 98, 130
Blocking, 31–35, 57n1, 67, 82, 90, 95, 98, 109, 131, 132
Body development, 16–17, 21, 45, 131; *see also* Strength
Body language, 102
Body stillness, 19, 35, 57
Breaking a board, 27
Breathing, proper, 8, 11, 21, 111
Breathing system: strikes to, 32n2, 39, 50, 54, 94, 95, 97, effect of, 27, 59; vulnerability of, 7, 8, 66, 67, 96; *see also* Solar plexus
By-standers, lack of help from, 3, 12, 109

Cane/crutch as weapon, 4, 141
Car as danger zone, 8, 103
Center line of body, 19, 23, 24, 27, 37, 44, 45, 49, 81, 82, 85
Centering, 19, 36, 48, 49, 50, 52, 64, 81
Chamber position: elbow, 49, 50, 51, 52, 93; hand, 22, 24, 26–28, 30, 45, 73; leg, 35–38, on the ground, 40, 41, 42, 110 (*see also* Striking, from the ground); return to, 24, 26–28, 30, 36–38, 45, 49, 50, 52, 63
Chen, William, Master, 144
Chin, striking under, 26, 52, 56
Chin-ups, 17

Choke attack, 74–78, 85–86, 115
Close-in techniques, 46, 53, 68, 75, 76, 117
Closed-fist position, 48, 49
Cocaine, 95
Combinations, 5, 7, 8, 19, 37, 96, 108, 111,
    115; empty-hand, 65–78, 94, 109; leg
    and foot, 109; sitting, 92–93, 94; see
    also Key chain weapon,
    combinations with
Commitment, 93, 124
Concentration, 13, 18–19, 24, 31, 64, 103,
    109, 132
Confidence, 27, 98, 118
Confrontation, 6, 13, 15, 59, 102
Contact sparring, 98
Coordination, 70, 131
"Cursing" attack, 8, 90–91, 96, 109

Danger zones, 99–108; banks, 103, 104;
    cars, 8, 103; elevators, 8, 80n2, 99–101;
    front door, 101–02, 126, 136, 137;
    hitchhiking, 105; hotel rooms,
    105–06; jail, 107–08; the street,
    102–03; traveling, 106–07
Dating, 136–40
Death as result of strike/kick, 39, 43, 44, 58
Dexterity, 84, 131, 142
Diet, 16
Disarming, 142
Discipline, 13, 15, 144
DMT (drug), 95
Dogs for protection, 127–29
Dojo (temple school), 12, 110n2
Door chain, 127
Drug users, characteristics of: "Down"
    user, 95–96; psychedelic user, 95;
    "Up" user, 95
Drugs, 95–96, 106–07, 134–36; dosing with,
    135, 136
Duncan, Ronald, Master, 142

Elbow, 4, 57n2; position/movement,
    22–24, 26–27, 43, 45, 81–82; as
    weapon, 53, 117
Elbow striking, 19, 39, 48–56, 68, 78; to
    breathing system, 67, 92, 94;
    downward, 50–51, 55; to head, 48–49,
    54; to rear, 49–50, 54; to side, 52–53,
    56; upward, 51–52, 56
Elevators as danger zones, 8, 80n2, 99–101
Embarrassment, 91–94
Empty-hand strikes/combinations, 8,
    65–78, 81, 83, 94, 103
Exercise, 16–17, 131

Eyes, 27, 46, 86; developing and training,
    19, 45, 47, 78, 131; strikes to, 7, 43, 94,
    103; vulnerability of, 7, 43–44, 116

Face: strikes to, 26, 27, 29, 30, 33, 39, 53, 56,
    58, 60–61, 63, 78
Falling, 8, 40, 42, 109; see also Striking,
    from the ground
Favoring one side in practice, 64
Fear, 11, 42, 91, 108, 111, 115, 119; dealing
    with, 6, 20
Fears, 3, 6, 8, 9, 20, 102
"Figure eights" with key chain weapon,
    81–82
Finger jabbing, 7, 8, 43–47, 75–76, 78, 96,
    116–18, 123, 139
First aid, 110
Flexibility, 78
Focus, 44, 58, 64, 67, 77, 116
Foot: kick to, 37, 72, 93; striking with, 19,
    57
Forced entry to home, 126
Forearm, 23, 31, 40, 45
Form, 16, 18–19, 24, 57, 65, 70, 74, 142, 143
Front door as danger zone, 101–02, 126,
    136, 137

Getting away from an attacker, 3, 6, 7, 12,
    14, 27, 86, 91, 135; see also Running
    away
Goju karate: Chinese, 144; Nisei, 144;
    USA, 28, 143, 144
Groin, 7, 19, 35; strikes to, 29, 33, 39, 53,
    57n1, 58–63, 76, 86, 94, 117, 123, 132
Ground fighting, 8, 60, 63
Guile, using, 11, 42, 94, 96, 107, 110, 116–18
Guns, 13, 127

Habits, breaking bad, 18, 63–64
Hallucinogens, 95
Hand, 16, 19, 108; in blocking, 31–33;
    guarding, 37, 67, 68;
    position/movement, 22–24, 26–27,
    37–38, 44, 48–52, 57n1, 67, 72; as
    weapon, 43–45
Hand signals to dog, 129
Handicapped, the, 4, 141
"Hanging technique," 28, 63, 64
Head, 8; strikes to, 57n1, 82; see also Face,
    Vulnerable areas
Head grip, 49, 54, 57n1, 58, 61, 62, 77
Heel striking, 32n3, 35–39, 42, 74; from the
    ground, 40–42, 117
Heels, 4, 37

Heroin, 95
High heeled shoes, 76, 108–09
Hip, 45, 60; movement of, in elbow strike, 54, 67, 70
Hitchhiking, 105
"Hog" (psychedelic drug), 95, 136
Hotel room as danger zone, 105–06
Hysteria, 107, 111

Injuries in practice, preventing, 28, 30, 46, 61, 132
Interrogation and fingerprinting, 107
Intuition/natural instinct, 99, 102, 136
"Iron will," 15–16, 109–10

Jail as danger zone, 107–08
Jeet Kune Do, 43, 44, 124n3, 143
Jogging, 16, 128
Jujitsu, 142
Jump Into Shape (Filson and Jessup), 16, 110
Jumping jacks as warm-up, 21
Jumping rope, 16, 17, 21, 131

Karate, 14, 16, 28, 98, 109, 118, 130, 143; Chinese Goju, 144; Nisei Goju, 144; USA Goju, 28, 143, 144
Karate Dojo, The (Urban), 143
Kau See (the "Monkey Master"), 60
Key chain weapon, 4, 8, 9, 11, 79–86, 90, 92–94, 97, 99, 102, 115, 141; combinations with, 101; how to make, 79–80; ready at hand, 103, 105, 106, 127, 140; stabbing with, 85–86, 93; striking with, 82–85, 93
Keyiii, see "Yell of spirit"
Keys/locks, 125–26
Kicking, 18, 36, 63, 65, 71, 73, 81; chamber position for, 35; from the ground, 41, 42; to the knee, 37, 71, 93, 96, 123
Kidney: strikes to, 26, 30, 55, 60, 62
Knee, 4, 24, 39, 45, 58; flexed position, 22, 35, 44, 46, 57, 76; strikes to, 37, 38, 71, 86, 93, 96, 110, 123; vulnerability of, 7, 42, 57n2, 71
Knee striking, 19, 57–63, 77, 94; double, 58, 61; to groin, 32n3, 117; "monkey knee," 59–60, 62, 63, 78
Knuckle push-ups, 16, 108
Kung fu, 143

Lau, Jason, Master, 143
Lee, Bruce, Grand Master, 11, 20, 43, 44, 112, 124, 143

Leg checking, 37–38, 71, 74
Legs, 8, 18, 22; see *also* individual strikes and kicks
Living alone, 125–29
LSD (drug), 95, 135

Marijuana, 107, 136
Martial artists, 6, 7, 16, 34, 142–44
Martial arts, 5, 12, 21, 91, 108, 113, 124; code, 6, 111; schools/programs, 16, 98, 118, 134, 141; study of, 7, 13, 142, 143; styles, 142–44; training, 5–6, 9, 98, 130–36, 143
Masters, 20, 142–44
Meditation, 21
Mental exercise/workout, 101, 108, 111, 141
Mescaline, 95, 135
Molesters, 91, 93, 132
Moment of truth, 5, 111–13, 119
"Monkey knee, the", 59–60, 62, 63, 78
Motion, flowing, 29, 36, 45, 57
"Moving rings, the," 47
Muggers, 3, 80, 86, 99, 101–04, 140
Murder, 3, 103, 118

Neck, back of: strikes to, 30, 55
Ninjas (assassins), 142
Ninjutsu (the art of stealth), 142
Nisei Goju Karate, 144
Nunchakas, 11, 142

Obosan, The, 144
Okinawa Te (style of martial art), 142

Pain, 27, 43, 53, 94; inflicting on attacker, 7, 8, 11–12, 43, 65, 68–69, 71, 91, 115; insensitivity to, of drunk and drug user, 94–95; tolerance, 16, 110
Palm heel strike, 17, 21, 22–35, 69, 71, 78; to breathing system, 94, 122–23; double, 25, 26–28, 29, 30, 122; to face, 63, 68, 72–73, 76, 93; variations, 25–28; see *also* Shove shock
Paralysis as result of strike, 26, 30
Peterson, Sue, 16–17
Pinky finger, breaking, 92
Pocketbook, carrying, 101, 102, 140
Police, 102, 126, 127, 135; confrontations with, 107; handling of rape reports, 9, 105, 114–15
Posture, 45
Power, 6, 14, 27, 38, 50, 73; source of, 22, 24, 41, 45

Practice, 19–21, 27, 30, 33, 35, 58, 65, 70, 82, 84, 85, 143; barefoot, 109; basic rules, 18–19; at full speed, 18–20, 24, 26, 28, 36, 38, 45–46, 49–53, 57, 61–62, 65, 74, 78; importance of, 4, 6, 15–16, 113, 117; screaming during, 20–21, 24, 26, 57, 74; in slow motion, 24, 26, 28, 36, 38–39, 45–46, 49–53, 57, 61–62, 78, 86; see also Target, contacting in practice
Programming to react, 6, 30, 65, 78
Protecting others, responsibility for, 12–13
Psychedelic drugs, 135
Pull-ups, 17
Push-ups, 17, 30, 131; see also Knuckle push-ups

Rape, 3, 5, 9, 11, 41, 44, 79, 90, 95, 103, 105, 107, 114–24, 136; in coed dorms, 140; "friendly" 14, 119–24, 140; at his house, 139; laws, 115; medical evidence in, 114–15; preventing, 118–19; unreported, 127
Rapist, 99; armed, 115, 117–18; unarmed, 115–17; vulnerability of, 116–18
Reacting to men on street, 90–91
Reflex action, 6, 70, 78
Repetitions, necessity of, 18, 19, 27; see also individual strikes and kicks
Ribcage, 22, 23, 24, 26, 43, 45, 50, 82
Ribs, strikes to, 29, 30, 60, 62, 63
Robbery, 5, 9, 12, 41, 79, 127
Roldan, Wilfredo, Sensei, 144
Ruiz, Frank, Master, 144
Running away, 5, 7–8, 16, 41, 69, 73, 77, 96, 116–18, 132; see also Getting away

Saying "no," 14, 88–90, 94, 121–23, 139, 140
Schizophrenia, 97
Screaming, 6, 20, 99, 102, 111; as martial art technique, 5, 6, 20, 68, 75, 78, 85, 115; see also Practice, screaming during; "Yell of spirit"
Searched, being, 107–08
Security, home, 125–27
Self-confidence, 4, 124, 132
Self-defense, 3–14, 16, 18, 19, 27, 44, 59, 64–66, 70, 77, 78, 105n1, 108–10, 113, 117, 119, 123–24, 132–33, 140–41; from the ground, 8, 40–42, 53, 63, 85–86, 109–10, 117
Self-defense training for women, 20–21, 98, 109, 115, 118, 130, 134, 140; handicapped women, 4, 141; objection of men to, 13–14; senior citizens, 3–5, 16, 115; teens, 115, 134–40; young girls, 13, 130–34
Self-discipline, 15–16, 22, 132
Senior citizens, 3–4, 140–41
Shin bone, kick to, 37, 42, 72
Shock, 43, 68, 69
Shoulder grip, 57n1, 59, 61, 62, 76
Shoulders, 17, 23, 24, 45, 57, 131
Shove shock, 26, 28–29, 94–95, 122n2, 123, 136
Slow motion, 18–19, 95; see also Practice, in slow motion, and individual strikes and kicks
Solar plexus, 19, 23, 45, 48; strikes to, 26, 27, 29, 32n2,3, 33n4, 53, 56, 94, 103
"Speed" (drug), 95
Speed (of strike), 4, 65, 69, 77, 78, 91, 93
Spine, 59, 67; strikes to, 55, 58–60, 62–63
Spray bottle of ammonia weapon, 86, 106, 127
Stamina, 96, 131, 140
Stance, 24, 38, 45, 46; shoulder-width, 22, 29, 62, 85, in blocking, 31–33, in elbow striking, 48, 54–56, in finger jabbing, 44, 46, in heel kicks, 35–37, in knee striking, 57, 58, 60, in leg checking, 37–38
Standing leg, 35, 37, 76
Stomach, 24, 54, 58; strikes to, 26, 31–32, 39, 51, 55, 59–60, 62–63
Stomping, 37, 38–39, 72, 93
Strangulation, 74, 86
Streets as danger zone, 102–03
Strength, 4, 98, 110, 122; upper body, 16–17, 131
Stretching, 16, 21
Striking, 5, 7–9, 18, 31, 44, 45–46, 65, 75, 90, 91, 96, 101, 103, 116–18, 123; from the ground, 8, 40–42, 53, 63, 85, 86, 109–10, 117
Striking point, 19, 39, 58–59, 62, 63, 65, 81, 82, 101; see also Target
Striking range, 101, 115
Surprise, advantage of, 7, 14, 27, 64

Tai Chi Chuan, 105n1
Tai Chi Ghu, 144
Target, 26, 43, 45, 60, 63, 81, 86; contacting in practice, 30, 37, 46, 54; on ground, 38–39; seeing, 38, 53–54, 94, 109–10; see also Striking point
Teenage gangs, 9–11, 141
Throat, 74; strikes to, 26, 27, 39, 44–45, 53, 56, 86, 103; see also Windpipe

Thumbs, use of in eye jab, 116
Timing, 70, 77
Toes, 22, 35, 37; gripping with, 22, 36, 41, 44, 45, 57
Tongue, biting off, 64
Tranquilizers, 95, 135, 136
Traveling as danger zone, 106–07

Umbrella as weapon, 141
Unconsciousness, 101
Urban, Peter, Grand Master, 28, 94, 110, 114, 122n2, 143–44
USA Goju Karate, 28, 143, 144

Van Clief, Ron, Master ("The Black Dragon"), 144
Virtues, 117; saying the, 15, 21, 108, 136
Vulnerable areas, 7, 8, 19, 27, 30, 60, 63, 68, 77

Warming up, 15, 21
Weapons, 4, 8, 11, 24, 79–87, 91, 102, 117, 127, 140, 141; martial art, 142; see also Key chain weapon, Spray bottle weapon, Umbrella as weapon
Whiplash injury, 26, 68
Whistle, 11, 86, 140
Wing chun, 143
Windpipe, 74; strikes to 44, 46, 94; see also Breathing system, Throat
"Wise guys," 105
Working with a partner, 18–19, 28–39, 41–42, 46–47, 53–56, 58, 60–65, 70, 74, 78, 83, 85–86, 94
Workout, a, 15–16, 30, 63–64; blindfolded, 33–34; order of items in, 18, 19, 21

Yamaguchi, Master, 143
"Yell of spirit," 8, 24, 26, 36, 38, 41, 45, 47, 49, 50–53, 57, 68–71, 85, 86; importance of, 20; see also Practice, screaming during; Screaming, as martial art technique.

Zulu, Chaka, Sensei, 144